Boy

Boy

The Story of my Teenage Son's Suicide

Kate Shand

First published by MFBooks Joburg – an imprint
of Jacana Media (Pty) Ltd – in 2013

10 Orange Street
Sunnyside
Auckland Park 2092
South Africa
+2711 628 3200
www.jacana.co.za

ISBN 978-1-920601-16-4

Cover design by publicide
Set in Sabon 11/15pt
Printed and bound by Ultra Litho (Pty) Ltd Johannesburg
Job No. 001971

See a complete list of Jacana titles at www.jacana.co.za

In memory of
John Peter Shand Butler

19.06.1996 – 31.03.2011

'As much as I hope the book will help others, ultimately it forms a most important part of my healing and ongoing transformation.'

– Kate Shand, 2013

Acknowledgements

I had the strength and will to write this book because of the overwhelming support, love and patience I received and continue to receive from my extraordinary family, friends, and work colleagues. My therapist Midge, through accepting me so completely, helps me to accept myself; and Fikile, the woman who in the midst of her own grief managed to somehow keep me and my home together. Chantel has shown me what courage is and that I will continue to get up every day. I would not survive each day of work without her presence and care. She has walked this road and knows. Compassionate Friends and LifeLine – Sheila and Lorraine – helped me through the darkest, the deepest, and the most desperate times.

My mother, Helaine, asked me what she could do to help me. I said she could help by writing and sending me her memories of John Peter. She did, and they form an important voice in this story. Melinda, my friend and publisher, was very brave to suggest I write this book. My best friend Vanessa and dear sister Nina have been like two rocks, rock solid they have stood by me and believed in me and willed me to keep going. David, Laine, Annie and Ruby-Rose generously gave me the space to write.

And finally I want to acknowledge Lisa Compton who did such a wonderful job of editing my untidy text and Joey Kok for giving of her time so generously to proofread the final manuscript.

My deepest gratitude to all of you who have reached out to me – each gesture of kindness and care kept me anchored. I am here because of you.

1

I have a son my son is dead I had a son. It becomes a mantra and the words can drive a person mad. *I have a son I had a son.* Since Boy died I have read a lot of books about suicide and grief and the loss of a child. Much of what I have read affirms that I still have a son, it's just that he's no longer physically with me. My relationship with my son will continue although he is no longer here in physical form. *I had a son he was fourteen years old he hanged himself.* It's as though by repeating the words they will somehow become real. The words will solidify, and the full and truly horrific reality of this tragedy will penetrate. But somehow the mind – or is it the soul? – protects me, for if I am to feel the full impact of these words, how will I continue? Instead I get sent my grief in parcels that I can handle – just. What I can't plan for is when these moments will arrive. Sometimes it's random, when I least expect it. I feel the tears welling up, the twisting of my tummy and the clamping of my heart, and my right hand reaches up and tries to find my heart, where the pain is, so I can hold it, as though touching it will stop it exploding. And the terrible and terrifying choking-crying starts. I may be at the shops or walking the dogs or sitting at my desk at work or driving into the driveway, but most often it's as the aeroplane takes off and starts flying. This I can now expect. Perhaps it's when I am flying that I feel closest to John Peter.

An interesting thing has happened. I am no longer scared of flying. I am no longer scared of anything. If someone asked me to, I would jump out of an aeroplane with a parachute. There is no anxiety about flying whatsoever. It's almost as if – and it's not really a consciously articulated thought – I don't really mind if the plane crashes because (1) I will be with Boy and (2) the struggle of trying to keep together the pieces of this broken family and of my shattered heart will be over and (3) I will be free of the splinters of pain and anger that pierce and probe and I will no longer feel this loss.

And it's not just the loss of Boy. It's the loss of the six of us struggling and bumbling through life. My family – chaotic and loud and opinionated and rebellious and colourful and loving and a bit messy and rough around the edges. My children – Laine, Annie, John Peter and Ruby-Rose – and my husband, David. The big old sad house doesn't seem to fit anymore and I want to move into a smaller, cosier and more comfortable space – one that doesn't echo the loss. And then there's the relentlessness of life. It never slows down but keeps grinding on. Day after day I have to get up and face whatever life brings. Just showing up takes all the energy I have and some days there isn't enough.

The most challenging and painful part of all this is that the hugest thing has happened – and it doesn't get much worse except perhaps for war or other mass tragedy – and yet I have to put on my face and confront the world and drop Ruby at school and go to work and carry on and yet everything is different now. I am so changed, so altered, I barely recognise myself in the mirror. In fact, I hardly even look in the mirror nowadays, not caring much about how I look. These days I have a relationship not with the image of me but with my interior life. I hate that life has to carry on. When tragedy strikes suddenly and severely, as tragedies do, there should be an escape route. Like a Monopoly game: first turn left, take R5 million, and move to that pretty little cottage at the foot of a rugged snow-capped mountain with a small stream running in front and a garden resplendent with flowers and people overflowing with love and kindness to welcome and take you on your path of healing. Instead it's traffic and hooting, and beggars without hands, and taxis pushing, and shopping centres and fluorescent lights, and work deadlines, and homework, and therapies to book for children, and fear for their wellbeing, and husbands who can't be reached (or is it me who can no longer be reached?) and birthday lunches with friends, and on and on it goes. There is no way of saying, 'Stop. I want to get off just for a while. Let me go somewhere, anywhere, just not here. I can't be here.' Yes, there should definitely be a special place set aside for grieving parents.

This book is an attempt to understand and put into perspective what happened on that fateful day to my son, to me and to my family. I want to capture and frame the person who was and remains our Boy. Writing this book has been a bit like putting together a jigsaw puzzle. There are the pieces that fit together and a portrait does emerge. With John Peter there was no urgency to excel or achieve or impress or show off his abilities. He was separate, apart, non-committal. Without guile. Slightly incredulous. Often bored. Undemanding. He was shy and reserved, and this manifested in a painfully self-conscious relationship with the world. I know these aspects of him, but there are still pieces missing, and so a complete portrait will never be possible. I will never be able to complete the puzzle and this is the hardest lesson I have to learn to live with. There was the son I knew and there was the son I didn't know. And even as I thought I knew him, I now understand I hardly knew him at all. I knew him in a particular way, I spoke about him in a particular way, I responded to him in a particular way, but there were always hints of the other aspects of him – the parts of him that I didn't know.

I write down my recollections and reflections at my desk at work, on the aeroplane, in the early hours of the morning. I grab whatever free moments I have to write a paragraph or thought or memory as it comes to me. I've been feeling much stronger of late, yet now, as I write, the tears are flowing again. Writing is an act of sheer iron will to go back there, to that place of such deep raw pain. Is it the right thing to do? Do I need to revisit this now? Is it too soon? Does my soul need more time to develop protective layers before going back there? But I have committed to the writing and it seems as if I no longer have a choice. There is an urgency to it. I am being guided and the words flow through my fingers and I am back there. And it helps. The writing helps me to make sense, to order my thoughts, to try to understand, and to remember and capture him just as he was.

2

I hear David's strangled voice saying, 'Come home, you've got to come home', and I say, 'I'm coming... what's happened?' He is choking, strangled, and he sounds so strange, not like David. He somehow gasps out the words 'He's killed himself'. I say again, 'I'm coming.' I get up and say to the person I am with, 'I've got to go, it's my son', and I run to the car and get in and in my head I am saying, 'No no no NO NO NO NO NO NO'. That's all that's going through my head: 'NOOOOOO'. I drive home somehow, the words still pounding in my head, there's been some misunderstanding, this isn't happening, NO NO NO... I am five minutes away – and then as I drive up to the house I see the gate is open. In the driveway David is on the cellphone, Annie is holding Ruby, and Fikile and Grace are on the front lawn and I know that it isn't *no*, it is *yes*. This has happened. But I can't quite comprehend what this 'Yes, it's happened' means. *My son is dead*. And I fall out of the car and fling myself on the ground and I scream – a blood-curdling scream of unrestrained anguish that reverberates across the neighbourhood and into the universe, where I am certain it still echoes – a mighty roar of mother loss. I am all animal – wild, I am all wild animal.

Fikile, our domestic worker, and Grace, the domestic worker from next door, lift me gently and help me to my bedroom. I let them. They lay me on the bed and I look up at that them and ask, 'Is it true?' and I will never forget those two gentle, kind black faces of the women who also love my Boy – slowly and sadly they nod their heads. And I cry uncontrollably.

Eventually I say, 'Somebody phone my mother.' What I say to her I don't remember. I think I say, 'You've got to come now' and she says, 'I am coming'. And then the only other person I want to phone and want to be with is Chantel, my work colleague. Her son died in a car accident five years previously – she will understand and know – I want her there, I want somebody there who will know. And I phone her and she says, 'I am coming.'

Then someone comes in and says that a friend is taking Ruby, my six-year-old. I say no, she must say goodbye to her brother first. And somehow I get up and take Ruby by the hand and start moving as if in a dream to the back of the house (how did I know where he was?). A friend asks, 'Are you sure you want to do this, Kate?' I have never been more certain of anything. Ruby has to see her brother dead and she has to kiss him goodbye. And so Ruby and I bravely keep walking, scared, holding hands, not knowing what we will find. Down the back stairs and there Boy lies. Grace has covered him with a blanket – to protect him – so he won't get cold. Ruby and I sit next to him and I ask for a candle. A small stub of a candle is brought down by someone and we light it. And he looks so peaceful lying there, as if he is only sleeping. But he isn't. He is dead. He has hanged himself. Do I know yet what he has done? The detail doesn't seem to matter. As I sit down next to him the first thought that comes to me is, *You've really fucked up this time, Boy*. And the knowing comes from a deep part of me. For a moment I dip into the deepest part of my intuition, my soul, my spirit and speak to him and *know* that this isn't what he meant to do and that it is a fuck-up. It is a monumental and the most tragic fuck-up. For the briefest moment before my mind gets in the way – while my heart is the most raw and open and accessible it has ever been – I know this is an accident. He didn't mean to do this – he meant to do something, but not this. But what does it matter what my heart tells me? *My son is dead*.

3

The blanket covering him is pulled up over his mouth. I gently pull it down and see that it was covering his mouth because his tongue is sticking out, and I quickly cover him again so that he looks unharmed and peaceful. Ruby is crying but I don't think she really knows what is going on. I tell her to say goodbye and she gently kneels over him and gives her brother a goodbye kiss. I don't think she realises that this will be the last time she will see him or touch him. And she is taken off for the rest of the evening – to protect her, I think.

I sit there for a long time. Just Boy and me and the candle flickering. *We're meant to be on our way to a restaurant of your choice for a burger or a steak or whatever you want*, I think as I look at him, touch him, stroke his hair. *I'm meant to be trying to get you to talk so I can understand what's going on with you so we can fix it.* Not this. Has this happened? Is this me sitting by myself next to my son's dead body? Chantel comes and we cry in each other's arms. Other people come and go but I don't remember much. Not only does he look so peaceful lying there, as if he's just sleeping and will wake up at any moment, he looks just like me.

I wait there for Laine to get home. I want to be with him when she gets back. She is working and a neighbour goes to fetch her. I know she is home because I hear her screaming as they tell her what has happened. She screams with the same 'No no no no' echoing my screams from earlier. She comes rushing to me and we cry and cry and cry, holding each other tight.

Then I hear Annie shouting at the police because they have put up yellow tape up as if this is a crime scene. As if my son has committed a crime by committing suicide. Or perhaps we are the criminals? Maybe we have done wrong? Broken one of nature's laws by rearing a son who takes his own life? Annie is so angry with the police. They just stand around close to us, watching us, their walkie-talkies jarring and interrupting us – so invasive as we try to say goodbye and just be with him, the three of us. Eventually we go upstairs. I ask Fikile to sit by him and not to leave him alone. David asks the same of his long-standing friend Mark. Fikile and Mark keep watch for the rest of the night. He mustn't be left alone.

I leave my son's body with his two caretakers and move as if through a thick fog up to the kitchen and sit down at the table. I sit in a state of disbelief. I am numb. I operate on automatic pilot. I smile at people. I say thank you. I let them hug me, hold me. I cry in their arms. Every known and learnt behaviour is sucked from me and I am left naked and raw. I am in a place that is so unfamiliar not even my name makes sense. I am no longer me. It's almost as if I have become someone else, except there isn't even a someone to become an else. In one moment I have become an alien. I move like a stranger in a world where the signposts have been removed. The signs I've used to navigate my way so far have become foreign and I cannot decode them. Is this how my son felt? Is this what shock feels like?

Everyone moves around me seemingly still full of life. Full of knowing what to do. Full of advice and words. Full of hugs. They know that tea is there and that it is to be made and that then you drink it. I hear their words. They give advice on undertakers. They are all waiting for the state photographer because my son has to be photographed. Is that someone saying that after the photographer the hearse will come? The hearse? A hearse is coming for my son? I am stuck in some dreadful nightmare. I will wake up. This isn't happening. What is happening? Everyone is being very careful with me. Are they scared I will disintegrate? Dissolve? They keep reaching out to me. As if by reaching out and keeping me conscious they will prevent my dissolution. And I am thinking that I am not the first mother this has happened to.

I'm sure I drink a glass of wine and I smoke a hundred cigarettes as I sit there with nothing to be done, because what is there to do? It comes to me that I have to do something to mark this moment. This is the moment that life has changed. Even before I've read any of the books on death and grief and loss, I know that from now on there will be a before and an after. But there is also a now. This moment stretches into an eternal now. I have never been so present to the now – I cannot escape the now. I am in it despite myself. This is now. This is the pain I am feeling now. I am pain. I am loss. I am grief. I am trauma. It cloaks me and enfolds me. It shoots through me. It shocks me. I feel my hand fluttering to my heart as I make sure it's still beating. I cannot make this now be something else. I cannot get up and walk into another room and turn on music and read a book. I cannot go onto Facebook and distract myself with other people's postings and lives. I cannot paint a painting. I cannot sit and daydream. I cannot go to work and keep myself busy with mindless tasks. I cannot drink a bottle of wine. I cannot go watch a movie or go shopping. All I can do is sit and feel what I am feeling. I know that on a deep level, in a fundamental way, I am forever altered.

I want to do something. I have to do something – something that isn't just inside of me – that will show the world and me that life is different now. I have to externalise this moment in some important way. I am different now. And as I have done throughout my life to mark internal shifts and watershed moments, I take my long black hair in my hand and hold it tightly to my head and ask my friend Gillian to get the kitchen scissors and cut. She says she isn't very good at cutting hair. She says she doesn't think she's the right person to cut my hair. But I know she is the right person. She does it because I ask her to and it feels right. It's not short enough, but that can come later. I want to shave my head bald. I want to wrap myself in orange robes, take Buddhist vows and walk the earth barefoot with a begging bowl. I never want to do again anything that I have done before.

David comes into the kitchen and says his agent is on the phone. The production company needs an answer. Is he going to go to the Cape tomorrow to start shooting the TV series or not? Oh my god, how can anyone have to make such a decision at a time like this? Our friend Graeme, all wise, sits in the kitchen and says, 'David you have to go. You have a family to look after. You have living children who need to be clothed, housed and fed. You have to go. Your son would have wanted it.' The mother of Graeme's children killed herself a few years earlier. He knows more than us. He knows that life carries on. He knows that in this moment we don't know this. For us life has stopped. And so David says to his agent, 'Yes, I'm coming.' A little later his agent phones him back and says that under no circumstances do they want David on set in this state and they will pay him out the contract. So for a while money doesn't have to be the force driving the decisions that have to be made.

People bring cigarettes, Rescue Remedy, tissue salts, bottles of wine, sleeping pills, tranquillisers, sandwiches – how do people know what to do? It's a human compulsion to do. While we are doing, we are. Some friends of the girls make scrambled eggs. I think that I won't be able to eat, but suddenly I am starving. As we finish the scrambled eggs, somebody opens the oven and there are two beautifully roasted chickens that Fikile cooked earlier. We laugh. The undertaker is phoned by someone, the photographer comes and the state mortuary van eventually arrives to collect John Peter's body. I am upstairs. I don't want to know when they drive off with my boy. I must protect myself from drama. I don't know how I am going to react if I stand there and watch my son's body being lifted into the van and then see the van drive away. I don't know how I am going to react to anything. Something else takes over. Somehow I know I must protect myself. That this is just the beginning.

Finally people start leaving. They return to the safety of their homes, where everything's still in place, where life still makes sense, and when they wake up in the morning they will count their children and they will all still be there, safe and sound. They go home with the relief of knowing this hasn't happened to them. And then it's just David, Laine, Annie and me. A while later Ruby comes home and she finds Boy's jacket – my work-branded jacket that JP wore every day for the past month or so – and she puts it on, wrapping her little body in it, inhaling her brother, covering herself with her brother, and crawls into our bed and goes to sleep.

Meanwhile we wait for our neighbour to bring my mother to me. At 2 a.m. she arrives and I fall into her arms and let myself be held and I cry. And we sit up for the rest of the night – Mom, Laine, Annie and me. We don't want to sleep. I think I will never ever sleep again. How can I do something as normal and ordinary as sleeping when my son has gone to sleep forever, never to awaken again?

David takes a pill, I think, and goes to bed with Ruby. Only then do I remember all the people I have to phone: my family and friends who haven't yet been told what has happened. Annie is the self-appointed messenger and makes the early-morning calls. Anything to be useful, to keep busy, to repeat the words again and again, hoping that by saying them over and over either the words will somehow prove not to be true or she will fully comprehend what has happened. She phones two of my closest friends, Sue and Melinda. It's still dark, but they get in their cars and come to us immediately. We phone my uncles, and they come too. Why didn't I think of phoning them earlier when I needed someone to take charge? Anyway, they are here now.

We sit in the dark and then the early-morning light. We smoke. We talk. It is a gentle time. The world is asleep. The night sky and the quiet provide a protective blanket. A buffer between what has happened and the stark light of day still to come. The moon and the stars gently watch over us. They are in their place. The cosmos remains as it always has. Watching over this sad, broken family. Reminding us that the earth will move around the sun and the moon will move around the earth and the stars will come out and twinkle at us. This too is just another moment, a moment that barely registers in the enormity of it all, in the timeline of eternity.

We are just another family – one of millions of families through time and space – who have experienced tragedy. But through the night and into the pink dawn we are the universe. Nothing else exists, except this moment and our confusion and loss – the full impact of which still awaits us.

And then the sun comes up, and those who are still awake go to sleep as those who have just woken begin to keep watch. I stay on the couch that night and for weeks to follow. I never want to do again anything that I have done before – nothing familiar – and although David and I are kind and respectful and attentive, we are on our own. I can't reach out to him. I don't even think of it. It is enough just to keep myself together. Grief is lonely. It cannot be shared.

4

I wish I hadn't let them take my boy away. If I had been more present, I would have asked everyone there to help me move him inside and upstairs, and I would have kept vigil by his body all night and in the morning they could have come and taken him away. I would have undressed him, and I would have washed him and dressed him again in clean clothes. I would have put his smart jacket on, the black blazer that he wore only once, when we went to Madame Zingara's and he looked so grown-up and handsome. I would have tickled his feet one last time. He used to lift those big, smelly boy feet of his up to me and say, 'Tickle my feet' – it was more of a command than a request. And sometimes I would if they weren't too smelly and sometimes I wouldn't. I always found it an unusual request, but perhaps it was his way of asking to be touched, the only way he knew how.

I would have taken a soft facecloth and wet it in a bowl of warm soapy water and wiped him down and made him warm and comfortable. I would have engraved, no, *branded*, every part of him into my mind for eternity. His hands, his fingers… I loved his elegant hands with their long fingers… I used to secretly admire them… and the curve of his lower back… and his big feet also long and elegant… his childish chubby boy face becoming more defined, more like how he would look when he became a man…

but not quite there yet… still in between… getting ready to shave…

I would have surrounded his body with a hundred candles. I would have gone into the night garden and picked foliage and flowers and covered him with the leaves and buds and branches of the shrubs he sat under as he thought his teenage-boy thoughts at the bottom of the garden. I would have burned incense and I would have just sat with him and helped his soul across to the other side and really felt and absorbed all that was him and all that he is now.

But how does anyone but the most conscious of parents know what to do at a time like that? So I just went along with whatever was happening.

Candles are lit that night and for the next two weeks we keep a candle burning twenty-four hours a day. If it goes out in the night, I am up immediately to light the next one. It gives me something to do, something to focus on; it is for him, it is for us. The flickering candlelight takes on cosmic significance, as if it can somehow help him on his way, as though it's lighting his path. More likely it is lighting our way – that fragile little flame showing us the way. A big responsibility for a little flame. But the candle flame does help. Even if it's only that it gives me something to do, something I can take responsibility for, a small act of doing that keeps from being totally consumed by the abyss.

Later, when we get back from burying Boy's ashes in McGregor, we keep the candle alight during the day. Whoever is up first lights it, and whoever goes to bed last blows it out.

Our house expands and at times seems as if it will burst with the people who come and go. Some are staying with us; some are friends, some family, some acquaintances; some people I hardly know or don't know at all. It feels as if the whole world is reaching out and holding me, forcing me to stay present and not disappear and be engulfed entirely by the shock and trauma of my grief. I am aware of my sister Nina and my close friends Jacques, Marian, Susan, Sue, Gillian, Viv, Hedwig, Guy, Manqoba, Melinda and Bridget hovering in the background – one or some of them constantly present as if they have a roster going, and when I look up and see them it is as if their presence is all that is propping my life up. I know they don't know what to do, but I am so grateful for their love and care.

No one who hasn't been there can fully understand how important other people were to me in that distant, deep, dark place of shock and disbelief. We all grieve differently, but for me people were and remain a blessing. They are an affirmation that I will be held through this – and that although so dreadfully alone, I am not isolated.

I look out the window and David is lying on his back with his arms outstretched on the front lawn, soaking up the autumn sun as if he is trying to get life back into himself. As if he hopes the sun's rays will recharge him. I notice him doing this from time to time – his way of staying connected? I find myself in the shower when it gets too much. I sit in the shower and feel the water pouring over me – my tears mingling with the water until I can't distinguish between the water from the shower and my tears. The whoosh of the shower water drowns out the sounds of my crying. And I draw energy from the flowing water. I step out with some part of me reclaimed. Those first few days are extraordinary in their liberation of ego and self. I do exactly as I am moved to do in any particular moment. No *should*, *could*, *maybe*; perhaps just a clear 'I want to do x, y, z...'

One morning soon after JP's death my mother runs a bath and gently leads me to it. She helps me to remove the clothes I've been wearing for days. I step into the hot water. She soaps the facecloth and she washes me. It is familiar. It's how she cared for me after Laine was born and my body was stiff and sore and torn and stitched. She washes my hair. She asks me what clothes I want to wear. I say I don't care, she can choose anything. Then she leaves me to lie in the bath for a while. She helps me out as my tears flow and she dries me and dresses me. She suggests I brush my teeth. Brush my teeth? Do I have to brush my teeth? This is what I did before my son died. It's different now. I brush my teeth because she tells me to, going through the motions like an accident victim in physio who has to learn how to make the smallest movements to start the healing. Then I go lie down.

5

Nothing feels right on the Wednesday night, the night before Boy dies. I am not feeling well. I fall asleep while putting Ruby to sleep with a story. I wake up at about 9 p.m. because the dogs are barking. I am not sure what is going on. I am disorientated. I look out the window and Boy is outside near my window. It is really odd. I ask him what on earth he is doing. He says 'Nothing' in that rather final way he has of saying it, which is often. He mumbles something about the dogs. Then for some reason I check my wallet for my debit card. David is going to the shop and I need to give him money, perhaps to get cigarettes? My card is missing. I search high and low and can't work out what has happened to it. David and Boy also help me search for my card. Finally we give up after looking in every conceivable place – even in my car – and I think to myself that I must have left it at Clicks earlier in the day and I will deal with it in the morning.

Thursday morning starts like most mornings, except I am up early. I've been getting up early rather often because I haven't been sleeping well. I'm restless with worry about John Peter. It's nothing specific, just a feeling, a nagging sense that all isn't well. I sit there staring out the window and worrying. As if worrying about him will somehow provide him with a magical layer of psychic protection – if I worry about him enough he will be okay.

I feel I have to do something, but no matter how hard I try to imagine what that should be I can't come up with a solution. It's a conundrum. John Peter has become a 'problem' I can't solve. I am not used to this. I am used to being able to come up with something – anything – that will shift the ennui that I sense is invading him and gripping him with pointlessness and hopelessness. What are my options? The home-tutoring centre up the road, where Boy did home-schooling for his final term of Grade 7? No – dagga smokers are too available to him, and anyway he'll be tested, it will come out positive and he'll get kicked out. He can't go back to his boarding school because of the cloud under which he left and he'd been so unhappy there. What about McGregor? Perhaps he could go to the McGregor Waldorf school and live with my mother? No, again a small village allows too much freedom to wander about with friends and smoke dagga. Clutching at straws, I move onto Murraysburg. He could stay with our friends there, but then what?

As I go over what I've written here, I see a pattern emerging. The only solutions that seemed to be available to counter JP's disease involved getting him out of Johannesburg. Those were the only options that seemed viable to me. And yet I didn't want him to go away. I had a strong sense that he should stay close to us and that he needed to be in the midst of his family, because we loved him and understood him and would look out for him. I sort of half smile – more of a grimace – as I write this. We understood him! How little we actually knew. All we had access to was the very surface.

Like an iceberg, he was floating along. The part of who he was that we could see was so little – most of him was hidden well below the surface. And if those with a spiritual context and belief system are to be believed and each of us has our allotted time on this earth – although I still can't get my head around whether this includes those who override God's will by taking their own lives – then perhaps in the end he was in the right place and I am grateful he was home.

The day that my son dies I sit at the kitchen window blowing my cigarette smoke out of the open window and reading an article in the *New Yorker* magazine. The article is about a young chess champion – an unusual chess champion because chess really is his passion and he refuses to turn it into a game of trained prior moves and so never goes into a game with a predetermined game plan or approach. I am reading it and thinking of JP, wondering if he were to read the article whether it might spark something for him. Even though it is the school holidays, he is also up early. He walks past me with a 'Hi, Mom' and goes straight out the kitchen door to the bottom of the garden, where I assume he will smoke a cigarette. He does this every morning. I wonder now, did he smoke dagga down there that morning? Every morning? I don't know. I've always believed that if he did I would have smelt it, but the girls assure me that smoking dagga out of a 'bong' neutralises the strong pungent aroma. So I simply don't know.

When he comes back up I tell him, 'I've just read an amazing article about this kid, a chess champion – do you want to read it?' He looks at me blankly. So stupid of me. Why on earth would he want to read a long article in the *New Yorker* about a young boy who is a chess champion? He doesn't even play chess! But I somehow want to infuse the chess boy's passion into my son. I want to set him up on a drip to fill his veins with 'passion', 'enthusiasm', 'motivation' and 'will' and watch him transform as these qualities move into his bloodstream and circulate through his entire body until they eventually reach the very core of him.

I get ready for work. There are lots of pull-up banners that have to be moved from the boot of my car to get the recently repaired spare tyre back into the very bottom of the boot. I ask Boy to help. He is willing and cooperative and does as I ask. It is quite a mission, but he pulls out the banners and puts the tyre in and returns the banners. He does it all without a murmur. And so I leave my home and four beautiful children and David, and I go to work.

At 9 a.m. I go across to Clicks at the mall to see if my debit card has been handed in, but no luck. So my next stop is the bank. At enquiries I ask them to stop my card and then to check whether there have been any withdrawals. I'm told there was an R800 withdrawal from the Engen garage up the road from us the previous evening. *That's so strange* is all I can think. The penny hasn't yet dropped. I leave the bank and phone home. Boy answers and I say to him, 'Something really strange has happened, Boy. Somebody used my card last night at the Emmarentia Engen and drew R800.' I am still naive although I think my intuition is trying to get through to me. He says, 'Oh' and then I start to feel decidedly uneasy. I ask him if I can speak to Annie and I tell her what has happened. And she says, 'Oh no, Mom, we went to Engen last night and Boy drew money from the autobank.' *Oh shit.* Annie says she will go and speak to Boy and find out what's going on.

'Boy, you are in big trouble,' she says to JP. 'Give me the money and whatever you bought with it. I will deal with the parents and protect you.' Boy gives her R400. 'Where's the rest of it?' she keeps asking him. He says that he bought junk food at the Engen. But as Annie later says to me, 'Mom, he couldn't have spent all of the money on Coke and chips and chocolate'. So after much probing and cajoling on Annie's part, Boy gives her a bank bag of dagga. He won't share anything further with his sister. Annie calls me back and tells me what she has found out, all the while trying to protect her brother and play it down. She intends to come to us once we have simmered down to a gentle boil and to give me what is left of the money and explain what has happened.

She tells me later that the dagga is hydroponically grown and that it is supposedly extremely potent, like rocket fuel. The girls tell me that dagga isn't like it used to be 'back in the day'. This stuff is really strong and it has hallucinogenic qualities. Later, when I am searching for clues about why Boy decided to kill himself, I ask a few people – regular dagga smokers – to smoke some of Boy's stash and they say it's great stuff. That there is nothing out of the ordinary or remarkable about it – it's just very good dagga.

I phone David. He is distracted because he is packing and preparing to leave for Cape Town the next day. He has a part in an international TV series. We talk about Boy – perhaps for the first time in a long while – and I tell him I am very worried. Why is Boy stealing money? The dagga smoking is getting out of hand, but the thing is, I don't smell it on him. Is it only dagga that is being smoked at the bottom of the garden? David says he doesn't smell dagga either. I say, 'What if he is taking harder drugs like crack or tik, because that we wouldn't smell?' I tell him how off-centre I am finding Boy's behaviour and David concurs. Now we are both very worried. But still I remain at work and David continues preparing to leave the following day. I tell him he must take Boy for a drug test so we know whether or not we can rule out drugs. We need to find out if there is something else in his system so that we can then deal with it.

I SMS the girls and tell them to watch their brother like a hawk. I don't want him to have an opportunity either to take drugs or to do something clever to make his test results come up negative. I don't want him even to know that he's being taken for a drug test. They agree to watch him. He stays with them all day until David can take him for the drug test.

They go to the SANCA (South African Council on Alcoholism and Drug Dependence) office in Sophiatown at about 2 p.m. David tells me later that everything about the drug test is a protracted affair, with JP resisting and saying he can't pee. After being taken off by the drug-testing person, he returns twenty minutes later and says he needs to drink a Coke, so David takes him to a nearby shopping centre and buys him a Coke and a packet of chips. Eventually the drug test is done and the result shows that there is dagga in his system. No surprises there – we know that. David and Boy get home at about 3:30 p.m.

But it's not like I haven't been deeply concerned about the dagga for a while now. I have been texting my mother, the girls, David, close friends. I am deeply concerned. I have this really bad feeling. It is only on that day that I suddenly wonder whether Boy is using harder drugs. It can be the only explanation for his odder-than-usual behaviour. And then David phones and says, 'It's only dagga' and I breathe a sigh of relief and think okay, so it's only stealing and dagga I have to deal with. I can finish my workday and meet the young Belgian researcher who wants a short interview about

Newtown, and then I can go home and take Boy out and try to find out what on earth is going on with him.

It's around 4:45 p.m. when I arrive at Scusi, a trendy coffee shop along the Parkview strip about five minutes from my house. I meet the researcher, and once we're seated at an outside table, I order a glass of wine to unwind before going home and having a talk with Boy. The young woman has interviewed me previously and we often bump into each other in Newtown, when I'm usually with the children. So she asks about them and I tell her all about them. The general chit-chat is followed by the interview and then I quickly finish my wine so I can get home. It's about 5:15 p.m. by now and I am going to take Boy out for supper. We'll go to a restaurant of his choice to eat a meal of his choice, and I can have a serious talk with him. I imagine he will suggest a Steers or someplace similar because he will want to cat a hamburger and chips. I look at my cellphone. Because it has been on silent for the interview, I see a lot of missed calls from the home phone number and David's cell. I am about to phone David when my phone rings.

I hear David's strangled voice saying, 'Come home, you've got to come home.' And then he says the words that are engraved into my head and my heart forever: 'He's killed himself.'

6

David is in deep trauma. He hasn't been downstairs to John Peter's dying place yet and the funeral is a day away. He can't go down. His therapist, Beata (not her real name), comes to the house to help him go downstairs and make peace with the place where he found his son.

Those of us at the house are invited to come downstairs with David and Beata. We all go down. Down the kitchen stairs, turn left and you are under the back stoep where there are pillars holding up the concrete slab above. The space is low and if you are tall you have to stoop to keep from knocking your head. Concrete tiles are laid neatly on top of the brown compacted earth. There are shelves full of old tins of paint, pieces of wood, jars of nails, and other bits and pieces that one day may have a use for fixing up or making something. David's set from his latest play is also there – a table and a bench. And the security gate that was cut down to neatly fit into the area below the stairs, and Ruby's old car seat, and the lawn mower, and spades and garden forks and other gardening equipment. There are no walls and the space is open to the garden. The wooden box Boy made out of old floorboards for Annie just before he died is also there, covered with candles and candle wax and flowers from the garden. It has become a makeshift shrine.

We all sit quietly on whatever we can find. David struggles.

Beata has her arm around him and gently encourages him down the stairs. She tells him softly it's okay and that there's nothing to be scared of. We light a candle. She asks David how he is and he says it is easier than he thought it would be. Beata says she regularly works with energy and she shares with us that the energy down here isn't negative or dark. It's a light energy. 'He left easily,' she says. But I think I know that already. I know it's not dark and heavy down there. I know I feel comforted when I sit down there. David looks dazed. Then he looks up and says, 'Look – the saw. I didn't put that there. Did he put it there? Did he leave the saw there to help me cut him down – or did he leave it there to cut himself down once he'd experimented and changed his mind?' The saw is too far from where he hanged himself for this last option, but the question remains: why did he leave it there? Did he think it all through that carefully? Did he think that his father would find him and have to cut him down and would need something to do it with?

The presence of the saw is one of the thousands of unanswered questions. Why, why, why did he do this? How could he have done this? How did I not notice that he was this unhappy? Was he that unhappy? How could he have been so unhappy? How long had he been planning this? Did he really mean to do this? Did he want his father to rescue him? Did he hope his dad would look out the kitchen window while he made his tea and notice movement through the foliage and go see what was going on? Did he hope Fikile would walk downstairs to her room and find him? Was he trying to get high from self-asphyxiation and not really planning on killing himself? Maybe it wasn't him – did somebody do this to him? I really did wonder about that possibility and asked the question explicitly: was he murdered?

The saw is yet another piece of the puzzle to confuse and addle and play tricks on the mind. If I think about it enough it could drive me mad. It's the not knowing. We sit there quietly and feel the space and the energy of our boy.

And then Beata, David, the girls and I walk back up the stairs and make our way to Boy's bedroom. The six of us sit there huddled together on the floor and we talk about him. And Beata says, in fact she repeats over and over again, that we must respect his decision. She looks around the room and says, 'What a typical teenage boy's room.' And it is. Magazine photos of women in bikinis, fast cars and graffiti on the walls, and on the table the old computer that was about to be thrown out and which John Peter rescued and reassembled in his room to play games. And there are his speakers in the corner of the room. Speakers he made for his car radio/CD that he so wanted for his fourteenth birthday. He built them himself. He knew exactly how he wanted them to look, and his father bought the wood and explained to him how to build the boxes, and Boy put them together and he varnished them and inserted the car radio speakers. And the messy school books. And his old sports stuff. There are cricket bats and tennis rackets and rugby boots. There are tins of deodorant and his wildlife books (he loved nature). It seems like a typical boy's room, but some deep part of me wonders if it really is. Or is it in fact what he thought a boy's room should look like? It can be seen almost as a gesture towards a typical boy's room. But perhaps all boys' rooms are like that?

He asked me if I could find a graffiti artist to paint graffiti on the walls in his room. I said I could, but that I really thought he was quite capable of doing it himself. I said I would get for him whatever he needed. I suggested he do some Internet research to find out what sort of paint I must buy and to find pictures that he liked and see how it's done. I told him I was sure there would be YouTube clips of how to do graffiti painting. I told him to go for it. Looking back, I don't think he really had the will for that – for such a big project. I wish now I'd found a graffiti artist and commissioned him to paint the picture Boy wanted in his room. Would it have made a difference?

In the early days of our deepest trauma and grief Beata opens her arms to us. Nina drives me to Beata's house and she takes me to her easy chair which she has set up in a horizontal position and there's a blanket and she lays me down and she says, 'Let it out, let it out' and her voice is so gentle and kind. I lie there saying 'No no no' and moving my head from side to side and I can hear my hair crunching against the stiff shiny leather. I want to feel it pull and hurt. The sound of my hair is amplified – it becomes louder in my head than the 'No no no' from my mouth. Hoping her words will penetrate the wall of pain, Beata says over and over: 'Respect his decision, respect his decision.'

7

JP's death brought about an avalanche of love. The generosity and compassion of family, friends, acquaintances and strangers during that first week is overwhelming. I want everyone to feel comfortable giving. I know the discomfort most people have with grief and I know each visit to us takes courage. To cross the threshold from the safe world into a world that has been rocked by loss and trauma isn't easy. I am grateful, and I want to make it easy. I know I cannot be comforted, so at least let a visit, a hug, flowers, food, a letter, a card, a photograph, a gift bring comfort to the giver. I hear a friend saying that she told people to stop bringing flowers as there were already too many flowers in the house, and I wanted to say, 'No, there can never be too many flowers. Let them send flowers – they want to do something, don't stop them.' But I don't. My mother tries to stop the flood of food as there's just too much. I want to say, 'No, don't stop them, there can never be enough food. We can give to the poor – they want to do something, don't stop them.' Another friend brings pomelos for days after Boy dies. They are huge and my mother peels them and I eat them and they are juicy and sweet. Letters and cards are dropped off all day long. I cannot remember how to get from point A to point B but I remember every visitor, every word written, every gift. I can list them right now… every gesture of care. We are given such generous donations of money that all anxiety about what we can afford and what we can't is alleviated in those early days. I can make the decisions that need to be made without saying, 'No, we can't afford to'. Each donation brings on another wave of tears as the generosity of my family and friends overwhelms me.

A Golf drives up to our gate, where a young girl drops off flowers and a note and then drives away with her mother. The note reads:

> Dear John Peter
> You were one of the sweetest guys I ever knew. You were always really quiet, so I guess no one knew what was going on. I sometimes saw you walking in Parkview and I'm really sorry now that I never said hi. I don't know why you did it, but I guess that I don't need to know. Seeing your cute smile put me in a good mood every time… I guess I loved you, in a way. Here's a pic of us at my party in Grade 3.

Did he know he was loved by a girl? Did he know he was loved by us? Did he know he was loved?

I want to mark the house, show that it is a house of mourning. I find a long piece of black fabric and ask my mother to make a bow. She makes a big beautiful black bow. And together we go and attach it to the front gate.

Wherever we look there are praying mantises, and then Sarah, Nina's daughter, finds a multitude of baby geckos in JP's bedroom. It's as if nature is acknowledging the enormity of this tragedy by sending us signs from the other side.

'Do you want to go for a walk, Kate?' my friend Susan from McGregor asks. 'Yes', I say, and she takes me up to Westcliff, where I can dance barefoot on top of the world. Dressed in white and wrapped in orange, I feel the grass between my toes and the breeze on my raw skin. Walking with me, Susan says, 'Let the earth's energy connect with you and move through you.' It's an alien moonscape up there, this once-familiar walking ground. I walk slowly and heavily, as if through a thick fog, but I move and I feel better for it.

'Do you want a massage?' my sister-in-law Rosalind asks David and me. Yes, why not? My body is stiff and sore from adrenalin and nicotine. Am I up for a stranger's intimate touch? I know it will help me physically even if emotionally I don't want to go there. The masseuse comes to the house and sets up her mobile massage bed in our bedroom. I remove my clothes and lie on her bed and surrender to her gentle touch. It is very strange but my muscles feel looser.

The inner circle of friends and family who have set up camp at the house are trying to organise the funeral programme. David's old friend Mark offers to lay it out. His eyes are bad and he has very little sight left, but he wants to do something to help. He tries. I read it and it needs work. My brain can't do it. I give it to my friend Andrew. He fixes it but by this time those involved are getting irritable. I can sense the tension – I have to leave. I go to the shower and turn it on full blast and sit in the corner and cry. When I emerge Nina and Rosalind have averted the crisis.

My best friend Vanessa shares some memories from those early days:

> Gillian [Vanessa's cousin and a dear friend to both of us] fetches me from the airport. She drives to your house. No one parks inside. 'Look,' she says, and points to the black mourning bow that you hung on your gate. She says a car guard just appeared and started watching the cars. He even had on a suit. David is standing on the stoep, staring out… I give him a hug. 'Go to Kate,' he says. You are lying on the couch, you smile when I see you, and very, very gently shake your head from side to side. I give you my stone and you rub it. The room is dark, candles are burning. Rosalind is helping Annie with her speech. Laine is curled up asleep on a cushion. I see your mom, she shakes her head, we hug. You take me downstairs to where it happened. And you say to me, 'I could never get cross with him, so I can't get cross with him now.' The day before the funeral you get in your car and we go with Ruby for a walk. There are so many, many people, Kate. You feel so much for David, that he had to be the one to find JP. 'No one should go

through that,' you say. There is a flurry of activity amongst the quiet. David is sitting staring at the fire, his mother comes, they embrace. It is heartbreaking to see the grandmothers. The morning of the funeral you retreat downstairs, away from the discussions of flower arrangements and transport. You get through the funeral and come home, and a crowd of teenagers are all downstairs when you get there. You say so politely, 'You are welcome to stay here, but please can we be quiet', and they respect it. You tell me afterwards of how Rosalind brought you the ashes in a basket filled with lavender and muslin. People bring pictures of Boy; the house is full. You lie on the couch, you won't sleep in your bed. You say to me, 'How can I ever do anything as normal as go to sleep and get out of bed again?' So you lie on the couch. You are very dignified throughout, as is David, still and dignified, but shocked, and you look in disbelief as you shake your head, small movements from side to side...

I hardly move from the couch that week. I only have to look up and someone is by my side asking me what I want – tea, coffee, water, whisky, a cigarette, food, whatever. There are people just waiting to help. The day after Boy's funeral, I look up and it's different. The house is emptier and no one is jumping up to ask what they can do for me, get for me. Where has everyone gone? I want a cup of tea. I'm going to have to get it for myself. I get up off the couch and walk to the kitchen. I fill the kettle. I turn it on. I get a cup out of the cupboard. I put the teabag in. The kettle boils and I fill my cup. I add some milk. I remove the teabag. I sit at the kitchen table and I drink my tea. With every action I don't want to be doing it. I want to be on my couch. I want to be looked after. I don't like the realisation. I resist it. But I also want a cup of tea. I'm going to have to make it for myself.

8

I decide to wear black to my son's funeral. A friend goes to a local dressmaker and arranges for her to make a black dress for me. My daughters also decide to wear black and my sister takes them shopping for their dresses. On returning they tell me how difficult it was to go into shops and have sales assistants ask them if they need help and what are they looking for and they have to say a black dress for a funeral.

On the day of the funeral, as I am getting ready, Susan asks me, 'Are you really wearing black to the funeral? Are you not going to celebrate his life?' And I am firm and clear in my answer: 'Today I am mourning my son, so it is appropriate that I wear black. This is not a celebration, it is a funeral. I am saying goodbye to my son. In time I will celebrate his life and all that he meant to me, but not today. This is the saddest day of my life. Today I have nothing to celebrate.' Later, at the service, I notice that she too is wearing black.

My brothers, Andrew and Hamish, come up from Cape Town for the funeral. I am sitting at John Peter's 'dying place', as Ruby refers to it. Sitting by myself, gathering myself, trying to find the courage I need to face this day. Soon my brothers appear and we take a few sips of whisky, drinking a toast to Boy. Hamish says, 'This is the saddest day of my life.'

Andrew and Hamish drive me to the church. We get there; there are so many cars and so many people. I ask if we can sit in the car for a while. I don't want to go in and have to sit and wait. I have my sunglasses on. I somehow summon up strength and tell my brothers I'm ready. I walk into the church. It's full. I see no one and everyone. I sit in the pew next to David, who looks dazed. I put my arm around him. My sister is on my other side holding my hand. I sit there in the pew and I close my eyes, as if shutting my eyes will somehow block out what is happening. Is this me sitting at my son's funeral? Who are all these people? Is that his coffin holding his body at the front of the church? It is a beautiful plain raw pine coffin with an elegant arrangement of flowers created by my mother. It is fitting and perfect and I wish we could go to a graveyard and dig a hole and bury him in that coffin. But I don't want to bury him in Joburg and it's all just too complicated to get him to McGregor where I do want to bury him.

The funeral service starts with Ruby and me walking up to light a candle that stands next to Boy's photograph so she too can feel involved and a part of the proceedings. Then Annie and Laine speak, and how brave and beautiful they are. They do their brother proud. Annie reads a few words that she has written about her brother:

> Lots of you knew him as a quiet boy, but behind that there was a charming sense of humour. In December my gran came home from the hairdresser with a new look. My brother casually walked into the kitchen, took one look at her and said, 'Sorry, my gran's not here', turned around and walked away! ... My beautiful brother Boy will be missed and never forgotten. He was our angel, who came but didn't stay for long. I am happy to have had an angel in our family. He will always be our angel. Love you, Boy.

Laine reads a Thomas Hardy poem, 'The Going'. I am amazed that both girls are able to stay so composed. Where does their strength come from?

And then David gets up to speak. I stand beside him. I don't close my eyes; I focus on David, on being there for him so he can get through this dreadful moment of having to speak a eulogy for his son, his only son. And he gets through it… just:

> … He was a quiet boy. He didn't need many words ever. We don't normally notice the quiet ones, but wherever he went, he touched people's lives. I know this because of the overwhelming response to his sudden leaving. Everyone who came into contact with him didn't have to hear him, they felt him, and he must have felt things far more deeply than we will ever know. Make no mistake, he had things to say, but only when it mattered.
>
> Even as a small boy and up to last Thursday, he loved the freedom of open spaces. He was always happiest in Murraysburg in the Karoo or in McGregor at his gran's house in the Boland, where he would go off on his own and revel in the unfettered and uncluttered spaces that they provided. He found peace there. He was happiest in those places. He needed very little.
>
> He left us a message. We found his rucksack packed with a sleeping bag, a blanket, a water bottle and a few provisions, and in his pocket was a list of things he needed to survive in the wild. He was planning a journey, an exciting adventure to the kind of peace that he knew and loved.
>
> He took up no space, but he filled up the gaps in our family. It is as if his presence and being made us complete. How to fill up that gap again, I don't know. We must find a way. Our instinct was always to protect him. He was loved by us unconditionally and without reserve. We truly, truly loved him.
>
> Today we say farewell to a part of JP and carry our love for him in our hearts forever. We have questions that will never have answers. We can guess, surmise and speculate, all of which are worthless. This quiet, kind and gentle boy made a decision that we must respect. He just could not find a place for himself here that was like the absolute joy he imagined it could be.
>
> We, as a family, continue sharing the love we have always had and, during the difficult time, the support and love that we have experienced so far.
>
> There are no words to express our grief.

The only way I can say goodbye is through William Shakespeare, who also lost his son. As Horatio says to Hamlet:

'Goodnight, sweet prince.
And choirs of angels sing thee to thy rest.'

They are the saddest words I have ever heard spoken.

I survive John Peter's funeral because, as I sit there, I shut my eyes in an attempt to block out where I am and what's happening, and there he is, my Boy. He is happy and he is smiling and he is flying. No, he is soaring. He is so free and light and easy. It's as if he is saying to me, 'Hey look, Mom, look what I can do'. I open my eyes and the vision is gone. I am back in the church and the pews are filled with people. I am happy the church is full. I want a proper funeral for my son. I want it done formally and correctly and with dignity. I close my eyes again as I feel the moment and gravity and tragedy overwhelm me. And there he is again. He is flying in the sky, free and happy with a big grin on his face. This vision is given to me. It is such a special and sacred gift. I am not imagining it into being. It just comes as if sent and I whisper to David, 'I can see him, he's flying, he's laughing, he's happy', but I don't think he hears me. I keep doing it: I open my eyes to make sure I'm in the church and then close them again when it gets too much and I'm back with him. I keep doing this and I don't hear what Tim, the priest, is saying. I just close my eyes and I am with him and I am flying with him and I feel such calm and know with such certainty that he is fine, he is just fine, he's going to be okay, I don't have to worry about him anymore.

My vision of JP smiling and free at his funeral is one of many fragile gifts that got me through those early weeks.

I asked Fikile and Grace if they would sing at Boy's funeral, but instead they arrange for Blessed, Rosalind's housekeeper, to sing because of the beauty of her voice. And she sings a stark unaccompanied hymn, a song to God, in Zulu, loud and passionate and exquisite and sore. For a moment it is just me in that church and Blessed's voice as it fills my emptiness.

And then the coffin is being wheeled out. My brothers get up and David's brothers, Mark and John, get up and JP's close friends get up and they walk the coffin out as the bagpipes play 'Amazing Grace'. And we follow after and then the coffin is in the hearse. Another surreal moment. There's a hearse with a coffin inside and it's my boy inside that coffin. And we all think: *This can't be happening – this wasn't meant to happen.* And I think: *This isn't happening to me. How can this happen to me? How will anything mean anything again?*

I stand at the back of the hearse to be near the coffin and I want to rescue Mom's flowers, but I also want them to stay where they are and I put my hand out so ineffectually, just to touch the coffin. It's a weak gesture of goodbye. I wish with all my heart that we could all get into our cars and make the slow drive to the graveyard and lower that coffin into the earth. I want to take a spade and pour the earth over his coffin and hear it thump on the raw pine. Instead I turn back into the church hall, where I have to face what feels like hundreds of people. Where is David, where are the girls? I don't know. I don't see them. Standing in their corners of the hall, I suppose, and I stand and I cry and I hug and I say thank you as some people struggle with inadequate words. Some say nothing – and I hug and I smile and I cry and I say thank you and I get people's names wrong and in the end the queue becomes a blur – until I see an unexpected face, a person who has made an effort to be there and whom I haven't seen for years and I break down a bit – but only a bit – and I carry on. Will it ever end?

We go back to the house, and family and close friends join us as we eat and drink and cry and laugh and remember. I will everyone to stay. I want to freeze this moment just as it is – I don't want them to leave. In this moment I am held, supported, protected by family and friends. And tomorrow? I dread tomorrow and the day after tomorrow and all the tomorrows after that.

9

This is the worst thing that can happen to a mother, this is the very worst, there is nothing worse. My thoughts are full of these words.

It is on the Monday after Boy's funeral that Anne arrives. An unexpected visitor who perhaps has been sent with a message. I see her and move as one mother moves to another who knows what it is to have buried a child. I say to her, 'You've been so much on my mind.' I am referring to the loss of her little girl who died eight years ago at just under the age of three. I was Anne's neighbour at the time.

I have been thinking about Anne because she is one of the few mothers I knew at the time of Boy's death who had lost a child. And I have been remembering how, in those first few years after her daughter's death, when I saw her I would wonder, *How does she carry on? How is she able to put one foot in front of the other?* I also have a very clear memory of a sign that was put on the driveway gate at Anne's house after the little girl died: 'Only family to visit please', or something similar. In my own early grief, that sign keeps finding its way into my consciousness. In the days and weeks and months after Boy's death, I become aware that grief is very personal and every person does it his or her own way. It's the one time when nobody can tell you what you should or shouldn't be doing. Even my own ego no longer controls my behaviour. It's as though I am able to connect to some deep part of myself and that is what directs me.

Then Anne starts responding to my 'You've been so much on my mind' and it is clear she is talking about something completely different. She is not responding to me and my loss, nor is she responding to her daughter's death. I feel like I've entered some kind of twilight zone because what is becoming apparent even to my garbled mind is that she is telling me that her son, Sebastian, killed himself on Sunday. That's yesterday! And she has driven to the morgue to identify her son and to my house by *herself*. I can hardly walk and it's been ten days since Boy died. It is difficult to absorb what Anne is telling me and to gauge my responses to it. I am confused and don't know what to say. She says Sebastian (the third of her four sons) had insisted that she take him to Boy's funeral. She didn't want to go, but he begged and begged and eventually she said yes and they went. I remember seeing her there – well, I saw her leaving as I walked out of the church. Three days later she went out to do the shopping and she came home and found Sebastian hanging from the security gate. He left a note that indicated there was no ambiguity in his intention. He had stood on a chair and kicked it out from under him. He was seventeen years old.

In this moment I realise that what has happened to me is not the worst thing that can happen to a mother. Here is a mother who has lost two of her children, and she is still standing, talking, driving. And in some way that I cannot articulate – it doesn't come to me in words, but through the mere fact that she is standing in front of me – I know I will carry on and keep breathing, walking, talking…

I feel that somehow Anne and I are karmically linked. She is never far from my thoughts and we keep in touch. She said to me that day, 'Sebastian was never mine. I knew he was never mine. You must understand that, Kate?' I always knew Boy was different. He wasn't resilient enough to suffer or endure the slings and arrows. He wasn't tough – he just pretended to be. And it's true, he was never mine.

10

Two weeks after the funeral we drive to McGregor to bury John Peter's ashes. I was not able to bury his body in its coffin, but the urge to bury him is still so strong. I need a grave; I don't want to scatter ashes to the wind. I want a proper resting place for him, one that won't be defaced. A place we will always have access to.

My sister arranges the grave site. She keeps phoning me and asking if I really want to bury Boy's ashes in the McGregor graveyard; she finds it a depressing place, grey and bleak and full of bright plastic flowers. But I love it there. And John Peter was happy in McGregor. He could just be himself there. And so that is where I want to bury him.

Sue lends us her large 4 x 4 and she takes over my little Getz. My mother, David, the three girls and I make the drive down, taking turns to hold Boy's ashes carefully. The dogs come with us too – we can't leave them behind, not after Beata told us that they know what has taken place and want to help and comfort us. Boy's ashes, his photograph from the funeral, his 'first 13 years' collage I had made for his thirteenth birthday, the thank-you cards we had printed using a drawing of JP's for those who had shown us love and support and kindness, and the large white candles all come along.

So we make the long sad journey down to McGregor. David and I tentatively reach out to each other, finding each other's hands, just gently touching, for the first time since Boy died. We spend a night in the Karoo town of Murraysburg, where we own a house and have spent many memorable holidays as a family. JP loved the place – he loved being anywhere he didn't feel confined and was free to roam the veld. Nobody really wants to be in Murraysburg that night, but it's a long drive from Johannesburg to McGregor and we need to get some sleep.

Early the next morning we are back on the road and that afternoon we arrive in McGregor to prepare for the burial. We meet with Billy – the owner of Temenos, a spiritual retreat centre – and ask him if he would oversee the ritual of burying Boy's ashes. The burial of his ashes is an opportunity for friends from McGregor and Cape Town to participate in saying goodbye to John Peter, and although it isn't going to be another funeral it's still going to be an emotional time. I have already learnt that with a sip or two of whisky I can endure anything. I prefer it to tranquillisers because I still feel awake and alert and not all dopey.

On the day of the burial, people from the village gather at my mother's house and we slowly walk down to the graveyard. David and I each hold a handle of the basket carrying our son's ashes, which are contained in an unfired urn specially made by Paul, my brother-in-law. I liked the idea of the unfired clay slowing disintegrating and the ashes and the clay once again becoming part of the earth. Everyone is carrying a stone to make a cairn. The day before we had gone to the river and picked a large stone of a suitable shape and size for a temporary headstone. On it I wrote in black khoki *John Peter Shand Butler 19.6.1996 – 31.3.2011.*

We go down to place the temporary headstone and make sure everything is ready for the burial of the ashes. I look to see who Boy is to be buried next to. I can hardly believe it – it's also a boy, and a June baby too. He was fifteen years old when he died. I find comfort that John Peter is to be buried next to a boy of his age – I imagine that their spirits make occasional visits to the graveyard to see what's going on down there and that they bump into each other and that they aren't so alone. It is only just before we leave McGregor at the end of the two weeks that I am told that the boy buried next to my son was also a suicide. I have goosebumps. He injected himself with his mother's insulin.

We gather informally around the small hole Paul has dug for the urn. Billy rings a bell three times – a Buddhist ritual – and then says a few words. This is what I really wanted – a simple, informal ceremony out in the open in nature. My mother reads a poem and close family take turns to cover the pot with earth. Irit, my foster sister, sings Kahlil Gibran's poem 'Your Children Are Not Your Children' as we each place our stones to make a cairn for Boy. There are beautiful stones and shells on that cairn. Later David goes back with river stones to make an outer shell to protect the cairn's beautiful centre.

I am not fully present that day except for occasional brief moments. I think I would have died a hundred times over if I had to experience fully my feelings in those early days. I get back to my mother's house and I operate on automatic pilot as I had at the funeral. I go out to the stoep with my whisky and cigarettes and don't move from my chair for the rest of the day until everyone has left. I am stuck there. And so people come to me – those who are comfortable enough to. I greet people and accept condolences as gracefully as I can. Lots of people are there for my mother and for my sister and of course for David and me. Some are old friends who have made a special trip to share in our loss.

I have learnt that few people can show deep empathy when you are raw and bleeding and open and in such intense pain. There were some of those people there that day in McGregor. I immediately recognise those who can face me, who can face my pain, who can feel for me in my pain, and I have those faces forever engraved in my mind. It's not pity and it's not sorrow that I see, and it's certainly not 'Oh fuck, I have to face this person. I really don't want to see their pain but I have to – so let me get this over with as quickly as possible.' I have become a master at recognising the truly compassionate and empathetic, those who are not scared to feel the pain and who can respond in an authentic and present way.

11

We return from McGregor to our empty house in Johannesburg, the saddest house in the world. And for the rest of winter the fire is lit every evening and we sit in the lounge and we play records, sad records. All the photos of JP are still hanging on the wall – and we sit there like automatons not sure what to think, say or do… where to go… how to move forward… where to move forward to…

He is still so present.

For a month or so after we get back, friends and acquaintances still come to visit, but eventually they have to get on with their lives among the living. We are better when somebody visits. It forces us to sit up and pay attention, to be present, to hear about somebody else's life and not just be captive to the internal monologue of guilt, blame, recrimination, anger, sadness and loss. Some visitors still bring food as if they sense that I cannot remember how to write a shopping list, what our needs are, how to cook, what to cook. Somehow our family gets by – we are close, we are kind to each other, despite our deep shock and trauma, which I think is beyond even what we consciously realise. It takes every bit of energy just to remember what the next thing is that has to happen. Often I forget and Ruby goes to bed without a bath, or her teeth aren't brushed in the morning. I can keep in my mind only one thought or one action at a time, and sometimes even that takes more will and determination than I possess.

Grief grabs you by the neck and it feels like it's going to throttle the life out of you. Grief leaves you gasping for air, with a heart beating so fast it could explode. It leaves you with a brain that no longer functions the way it used to – a blank mind overflowing with nothingness and emptiness. At other times my mind is so full of John Peter – the image of him, the smell of him, the touch of him, and the pain and dreadfulness and loss – that it feels as if I could self-combust. The thought that he's gone *just like that*. One moment he was there and I was talking about him and texting about him and worrying about him, and I was going to take him out and talk to him and try to get to the bottom of what was going on, and talk and worry and talk and worry – and now he's gone and what am I left with? 'What am I left with?' I scream at no one in particular.

The mothers at Ruby's school organise a winter uniform for her. They must know that I am unable to complete even the simplest of tasks. And the offers of help pour in – 'Anything – just ask'. But what do I ask for when I don't even know what my needs are anymore? *Visit me*, I want to say. *I don't want to feel isolated – just pop by and have a cup of tea with me. And if I want to talk about Boy, let me. And don't feel you need to protect me or give me advice. Don't comfort me if I cry – just sit there*. It seems such a simple thing to ask for – *just sit with me* – yet how difficult it is for most of us. We want to fix and mend and avoid and distract and gloss over and keep busy and be practical, but for most of us just to sit and listen – or just to sit next to somebody who is suffering – we are not brought up to be able to do this easily, if at all.

I find a few men I can talk to about John Peter. That they are not scared of talking about him is such a comfort. They remember vividly being fourteen years old. They can remember the impossibility of the age – of feeling useless and hopeless and angry and confused and overwhelmed. They can remember having thoughts of ending it all – it seems the difference is that JP acted on his. For a boy of little action and who constantly needed encouragement, I can only wonder at it all.

The mothers don't like to hear me talk. Instead of just listening, they want to jump in and tell me it isn't my fault – that I mustn't feel guilty – before I barely have the words out. It's as if by them saying to me, 'You are not guilty, you are not to blame', they are somehow absolving themselves of the perennial guilt and blame of motherhood.

But I need to talk. By talking I think I may grasp some elusive truth. If I hear myself say the words, some meaning may emerge from the thick dank fog. And that's why the group work I have come to participate in has been such a balm. I sit and listen to the other members of the group talk about their blame, recrimination, guilt and anger – and I can see how pointless it is. I want to say to them, *Can't you hear how ridiculous you sound when you blame yourself for the suicide of your brother/husband/father?* And I laugh at myself because when it is my turn to talk I can hear my words and they are no different. My words echo my deepest fears – did I somehow cause this?

This is what complicates the grieving when a loved one dies by his or her own hand. I don't think it's humanly possible to come to a place of complete resolution about a suicide. The feeling of self-blame may diminish and may one day no longer occupy every waking thought – but does it ever really go away entirely? Would we be truly human if we could walk away from something like this? My hope is that my guilt and blame will transform into responsibility, for as human beings we are all responsible. I want to wake up, to become conscious, to be aware of how I am in the world and of the effect of my actions – not that my actions are good or moral or whatever, but that the actions I take are *conscious* actions, if that makes sense.

If nothing else, my son's death must *wake me up*. I want to become conscious and live the rest of my life consciously. I want to know myself. Honour myself. Well, this is my intention at any rate. I know I will stumble and fall, but I will get back up and try again – and that's all I can hope for.

I learn a lot from attending the groups: I know I am not to blame for my son's choice to hang himself. But I do take responsibility for my choices and my mothering – and I will learn to forgive myself for some of them, the ones I'm not so proud of. But loving my son with all my heart; feeling delight at watching him grow and become a man; worrying about him; helping him; asking him if he's okay, does he need therapy, does he want to try Ritalin or go onto antidepressants; encouraging him to make Annie's wooden box, to paint the kitchen cupboards, to chip off the horrid green kitchen tiles; tickling his feet; hugging him; telling him I love him; delighting in him kicking a ball around, planting his herbs, digging holes for me to plant my plants, keeping his sister company; gently nudging him along; appreciating his difference; supporting him when he needed so desperately to change schools – for all of that I also take responsibility.

I spend some valuable time with a wonderful older woman, an artist, whose son also killed himself. She once said to me in a very kind but matter-of-fact way, 'You will carry with you for the rest of your life the responsibility of your child's death – because as a mother we know our role is to protect our children and to keep them alive and we weren't able to.' And that's the truth… the uncomfortable truth. I wasn't able to keep my son alive. Me with all my life force and energy – overflowing with enthusiasm and a love for life; full of optimism, solutions, adventures, activities and ideas – somehow it just wasn't enough to keep him alive.

12

How did it happen, Boy? What went on that day?

I often go and sit at the bottom of the garden and, when my mind allows me to, I wonder what happened that fateful afternoon. Were you just sitting there smoking a cigarette, Boy? Me at work, Fikile doing the ironing, Ruby having an afternoon nap, Annie watching a video with a friend, your father coming and going. You knew he was going out for a haircut. Did you just sit there and think, *Fuck this, fuck them, I'm checking out*? Was it that simple? One minute you are sitting at your table at the bottom of the garden and the next you find yourself walking to that place under the stoep, compelled by a deep scream of the soul to stop the noise, the fuss, the chaos, the confusion?

Or am I being dramatic? You were never a dramatic child. Was it a calm, considered decision? Something along the lines of *I don't want to be here anymore?* Did you look at your options? No, I don't think so. You never did really. You'd get an idea in your mind and you'd follow it without getting sidetracked (unless it was schoolwork or a project and then you'd get very sidetracked). Had you decided that running away wasn't an option – it was too complicated?

You got back from your drug test at about 3:30 and two hours later you were found dead. The girls had asked you what your test results were. You joked back, 'Positive... for Mandrax', but then told them it was only dagga. You spoke to Fikile – she says you were jokey and chatty like you always were. She picked up nothing unusual in your tone or manner. Perhaps the thought had not yet crossed your mind?

The minister who conducted John Peter's memorial service at his school told the children that there's a five-minute window when you decide to kill yourself. In order to act on the decision, there are three elements that need to be in place during those five minutes: a motive or reason; a method or object to kill yourself with; and the right time and place, or setting. The minister said that because these elements are rarely in place all at the same time, suicide is like an accident. Not that I believe much of what the experts say. For who knows the workings of a soul or a mind that is ill? The fears, the dreams, the compulsions, the intrusions, the deep spiritual and psychological make-up of an individual? You did ask her for brandy, Fikile says. You looked in the kitchen cupboard in that nonchalant way of yours and asked, 'Isn't there some cooking brandy?' And she probably joked back at you and said, 'No, Boy. What do you want brandy for?'

Laine said goodbye to you and went off for her evening's work. And you went down to your corner of the garden and sat and pondered life… and, I imagine, death. Death as an escape, a release – without, I'm sure, understanding that death would be a permanent solution, not a temporary release from your situation. And I remember again how you would always say, 'There's a problem!' and we would try to fix it. And this time there was a problem, but what exactly was it, I wonder? Was there something specific you couldn't articulate or share with anyone in the world? Something you were so deeply ashamed of and humiliated by? Or something that had just got out of control and you didn't know how to get it back to the normal, to the ordinary?

Your father said to you that morning, 'Is there a problem, Boy? Just tell me what it is and we can fix it.' And you said, 'There's nothing wrong.' Were you stoned? I keep thinking of the dagga smokers I know and have known, and under the influence they are usually incapable of doing much of anything, let alone killing themselves. Being stoned takes the edge off. But my friend Melinda tells me that this isn't strictly true. For people with mood disorders, getting stoned can make them highly strung out, disturbed and paranoid. She says that she used to feel suicidal when she was stoned. Perhaps you weren't stoned at all, but the edge was back and that's what you were trying to get away from.

All these things go around and around in my head and I know I will never have all the answers, but I am compelled to keep asking questions. As if by asking and by looking at all the options – by thinking specifically of you and how that unusual mind of yours worked – I might get an answer, a eureka moment and I will be able to say, 'Ah, so that's why you did it. Now I understand.' I don't think the answer is as simple as 'he smoked too much dagga, got paranoid and hanged himself'. But what if it is that simple? What do I do with that knowledge? I was careless, I wasn't paying enough attention, my son slipped through my fingers so quickly, before I had a chance to do something.

My mother writes to me:

> Curiosity led me to the quiet hidden corner that had become Boy's place. There I found the scattered remains of some plastic containers. Mostly bottles, like large Oros bottles, and other big square-shaped ones. Some squashed, discarded half under the bushes. They had been rebuilt, cut into new shapes and melted into one another. Lots of crumpled paper and used matches and boxes lay about. There was an acrid smell. I knew this was the detritus of a dagga smoker and I knew Boy was smoking. But I was shocked by the overtness and carelessness and the extent to which it had gone. With my heart thumping and tears burning I gathered this evidence and discarded it.

That discarded stuff had got there quickly. It was a matter of months. I didn't go down there to his place at the bottom of the garden. I felt it would have been an invasion. He had so little privacy, and that place felt like his. Did he leave everything lying about because he knew he was in danger and wanted us to find the evidence of his dagga smoking so that we would stop it?

Those of us who are part of the living can never imagine that dark moment of the soul when nothing makes sense anymore and the only option is a release and the only way to release the pressure valve is through death. In the book *Suicide and Attempted Suicide*, Erwin Stengel writes about the ambivalence of suicide. He explains that the act of committing suicide is about wanting to live and die at the same time – it's not about either/or. He writes that those at risk of suicide and under tremendous stress do not know exactly what they want and it is 'unpsychological' to expect them to know what they want to do.

I imagine you hearing your father's car leave and knowing that everyone else is safely in the house. You did it while so many people were around. Were you hoping to be found before you died? Or did you know that it's seldom that you are left alone at home and so you took your chances? Were there voices in your head telling you to do it? Did you just casually get up and go under the stoep and get the straps that your father uses to secure the set for his play to the roof racks on the car – were they kept under the house? Did you have to go inside and find one and bring it down? Or did you just look around in that space under the stoep and find something you could use? Did you take the strap and knot it around the burglar gate and listen one more time for the sound of family? When you heard nothing, you then must have put your head through the noose you'd made and climbed onto Ruby's old car seat. Why, when it was so low, did you need to climb on anything? And then you dropped from it, using the strap – a mechanism that once pulled tight can't be untightened because it locks into place. Did you know all of this? Sometimes I wonder if you just wanted to test it out – see what it felt like – but then planned to undo the mechanism and start breathing again. But as I write this I remember the detail of the car seat – to drop you needed to get some height, if only a few inches, so that the mechanism would pull tight and that would be it.

But your father tells me that your feet were so neatly together when he found you that he doesn't think you jumped. He thinks you just lowered yourself gently and the tie pulled tight. Annie was told by someone that there is a pressure point in your neck that when pushed upon with sufficient weight leads to instant death. She finds this thought comforting. So do I.

How long did you hang there for before dying? How long does it take to suffocate?

There was no sign of struggle, your father tells me. You were just hanging there when Annie found you and David cut you down – your knees almost touching the floor. You could have reached out to either side of the burglar bars and held yourself up, or you could have tried to release the pulley, but was it too quick? Did you somehow succeed in hanging yourself in that small low place by knowing exactly what you needed to do? Was this premeditated? Had you, months ago, when you asked your father for the strap, already worked it all out? And then just like that – gone? One moment sitting at the outside table smoking a cigarette, the next moment gone? So quickly and quietly and certainly. Or was it an accident?

The mind plays so many tricks. I have gone over this a million times, and each time a detail is missing or conveniently forgotten so a new or different version of what happens slips in to confuse and enlighten for a moment – until something, a detail like the car seat, is remembered.

And what happens next? David comes home. He's had his haircut. He looks for Boy – he walks around the house calling for him and there's no reply. He'd done the same before going for his haircut and assumed that Boy had gone next door to his friend Thando. This time there is an urgency in finding him. David asks Annie, 'Where's your brother?' And she gets up and also starts looking – where is Boy? They all wonder. Then Annie gets a bad feeling. She says, 'I know where he is.' She thinks he's on the roof and he's done something stupid. So she goes out the kitchen door and down the kitchen steps, and as she turns to go around the right side of the house to the stairs to the roof, something catches her eye and she looks left and there she sees her brother hanging. And she screams a scream that David will no doubt never forget

– and he comes running and he sees his son hanging and he yells for Fikile to bring a knife. And he cuts Boy down and lays him on the ground and although he knows that he's too late he still tries to get some breath and life into him but it's futile. He's dead. And Annie goes to get Ruby in case she comes down, and she pushes every button on the alarm and summons every emergency service, from our security company to the fire brigade, the police and the ambulance. And she deals with them as they arrive. And then David phones me – I come.

13

What brought Boy to a place where death was preferable to life? What path did he walk from birth to his still-so-young fourteen years? Was it something I did or didn't do as a mother? Something David did or didn't do as a father? I have only questions and no answers. What I do know is John Peter was born beautifully and exquisitely at home.

It is a perfect painless birth and I am euphoric and empowered. My contractions start in the morning and I spend the day walking up and down the wooden passage that cuts through the centre of our old Berea house. I love each contraction and welcome the tightening of my uterus. I am not scared. I feel prepared for this birth. I am in control and in charge. This time I know my body will cooperate. It knows what to do and I am going to have a perfect home birth. I have never been more certain of anything.

The midwife comes to see how I'm doing in the late-winter afternoon. She gives me a pill to put under my tongue to help the contractions. She is aware that my previous labours were long, protracted affairs. There I am in my home, in the middle of a cold Johannesburg winter, preparing for a birth. There is a large fire burning. I am listening to my esoteric music to aid my relaxation. I am surrounded by friends and my sister: Mark, Irit, Sue, Vanessa and Nina. They come and go like any day in our Berea house. It is always open house here, full of friends and family and lodgers.

David leaves for his performance in *A Tale of Two Cities*, hoping to be back in time for the delivery. The contractions become stronger and I move to the couch in the lounge. I spend the next few hours rocking backwards and forwards on my hands and knees in front of the roaring fire. The midwife rubs my back as she murmurs comforting words to me, and the fire keeps me warm as I go deep into myself and enter what seems like my primal sacred place. There is no pain, it is just intense and enormous, and when I start feeling like it's getting to be too much I ask if I can move to my bed. The room and the bed have been prepared by the midwives. There are lots of black bags under the sheets and a heater and the midwives are quietly talking and their equipment is set up and the light is soft. Nina and Vanessa also come. I get onto the bed and ask for some pethidine. The midwife gives me a shot and I am able to relax completely for about half an hour and then I know it is time. I roll onto my back and Vanessa sits up close next to me and the midwife is saying, 'It's time to push'. I try to push but I feel so relaxed that I ask, 'Do I really have to push? Won't the contractions do the work of pushing him out?' The midwife says, 'No, Kate, you must push – push, Kate – let's get this baby out.' Vanessa joins in the pushing chorus and says, 'Push, Kate' as she holds onto my left knee. My sister Nina stands at the end of the bed with her arms folded, shaking her head as though what she is witnessing is not possible. She is wide-eyed and amazed. And I manage to push, although I don't remember pushing very hard. And out the baby slips.

I can't believe that I've done it. All by myself at home in my bed – without screaming, just gently supported – I have done it. I am so proud; I have never been prouder of anything really – not my master's, not my nice new job, not anything – but that birth... and then the biggest surprise of all – it's a boy. I burst into tears. I cannot quite believe it. I never expected to have a son. I always assumed I would only birth daughters. I had given little thought to a son. I immediately sense his difference and I love it. He isn't a small version of me. He is a him. I am so used to the girls that

I keep referring to him as a she or her and so I start referring to him as *Boy*, so it sinks in. I have a boy – a great big healthy boy. The midwife runs a bath and gently leads me there and I sink into the warm embracing water and she brings the baby to bath with me. It is a delicious and delirious moment. I am in my bath in my home with my baby boy in the bath with me. Afterwards I put on my new Woolies pyjamas – a complete indulgence because there isn't money for such but I used my Woolies card. I get into my bed and hold my baby close and watch as he finds my nipple and starts drinking hard and firm and fast – not like the girls, he knows just what to do. He sucks with knowing and strength and vigour from the start. It is a truly perfect birth. It is exactly what I want it to be, what I know birth can be. And he sleeps with me in that bed until we move to McGregor six months later.

I choose a home birth because I don't really have a choice. We don't have medical aid so we can't afford the private hospital route and the Joburg Gen is no longer an option. When I gave birth to Annie at the Gen, I had an uncaring and distracted midwife. There were no hospital gowns and no bedding. There was blood in the bath that hadn't been cleaned. I cannot afford a private hospital birth. And so even in birth as in his life, my son cooperates. He makes it easy for me. He comes into the world without any drama.

Vanessa leaves a message on my Facebook page on his sixteenth birthday: 'I just remember your calmness and joy and his black hair, and Irit's false eyelashes, and the little girls in bed, and the joy and happiness surrounding his birth. And there was this lovely calming music that was playing, and the date. X.'

He is born on 19 June 1996. It seems auspicious somehow, all those nines and sixes.

He was born at home and he died at home. He slipped into the world without making a fuss – he lived in it for nearly fifteen years without making a fuss – and then just as easily as he arrived he slipped out of it without much of a fuss. Quietly. There is a strange poetic symmetry in his arrival on this earth and his departure from this earth – both at home, both quietly, with barely a whisper.

But what has he left behind? He may not have demanded much

from any of us while he was with us, but his death has left each of us grappling and clawing our way to some sense and meaning. The aftermath for each of us is as if our own personal tsunami has taken place. Giant waves of grief and sadness engulf and overwhelm, and the threat of drowning in these waves is there. I come up gasping for air. I am confused and dazed as I try to do the ordinary routine things that used to come so easily, except now everything is turned upside down. Sometimes I float on the tidal waves and sometimes I hang on to whatever is nearest and cling for dear life and sometimes I can and sometimes it feels like I'm going to drown and that it's not possible to survive this. But then I do. The most ordinary of tasks take Herculean effort to undertake. Nothing has its place anymore.

It is ironic that through Boy's death, his absence, his loss, he has become the most demanding of children. He demands of me that I keep putting one foot in front of the other and the longer I do this, the more demanding those steps become – not easier, as some would imagine.

And then one day it's no longer just a matter of carrying on one step after another. The steps want to start doing the two-step. They want to dance a little. They want to take all the pain and all the trauma and all the loss and transform the mindless prison shuffle into steps that are more life-affirming. And then a little miracle takes place. Ruby puts on some music and she starts to dance and then she takes me by the waist and holds my outstretched hand and says, 'We're going to dance like Italians'. And we do what I think is her version of a tango and we march up and down the house changing direction and moving our heads dramatically from side to side and then an occasional twirl and we throw our heads back and we laugh. The music has stopped and we are now making it up as we go along. Just the two of us dancing and laughing. It feels miraculous.

14

All families have stories that are passed down from one generation to the next. These stories cover unusual events, such as immigration, fights and battles, secret love affairs, eccentric aunts, particular rituals, holidays, floods, droughts, births and deaths. It's often difficult to distinguish between the facts of lives gone before us and the fiction of those lives. After all, in any family story what is remembered, what is included, what is excluded, what is embellished and what is imagined is up to the storyteller. What I am sharing here are my memories of the family stories I've been told. They may not be strictly factual, but they are as true to me as any good story is.

John Peter's grandfathers, Peter Shand and Basil Butler, were men of few words. They were both reserved but with a sharp wit. Basil was always looking for a joke and loved to laugh. They were clever men, highly regarded professionally, yet humble. Both were born in the early 1930s and were very much products of their time. They were Cape Town-educated: Basil at Rondebosch Boys and my dad at SACS, and both went to UCT. And the similarities don't end there.

When Basil died not long ago, David and I spoke about him at length. Who was he and how did he grow up? David said that Basil never spoke about his father or his family life growing up;

it was as though he didn't have a father. Basil's father, Lesley, had been a racehorse trainer who won the Met. For a while the family were well off. Lesley was ebullient and debonair, a drinker, very entertaining and gregarious. But once the money ran out, the family lived in straitened circumstances. Lesley lost everything and died of throat and mouth cancer.

It was only when my father was on his deathbed that we got to know more about my grandfather, Cecil, because my father also never spoke much about his father. Were both Basil and my dad disappointed by their fathers in some fundamental way? Dad told my mom that he wanted nothing to do with that old bugger his father. And he didn't... ever. When my dad was dying, my mom went for a walk with his cousin Walter, and she asked for confirmation of the stories she had been told about my elusive grandfather. Walter said he was Greek and our surname should be Nicolaus-Courtelis. Walter said Cecil never really worked, and family myth has it that Granny refused to iron his white linen suits and so he had to do it himself. So a piece of the ancestry puzzle falls into place – that's why my dad and brothers have such olive skin and black hair. I wonder what else we don't know about that may have been passed down genetically. My father knew about his lineage, but he never shared the information with anyone, not even my mother. I was conceived on a Greek island and even then he didn't feel the need to share with his new young wife the truth of his ancestry.

Why don't I have my grandfather's name? Dad's mother, Iona Shand, but known as 'Granny' to everyone young and old, lived with us for most of my life. My father was her only son. She didn't think much of men, although she could flirt with them and bat her eyelashes even when she was in her eighties. Granny divorced Cecil when my dad was young. Then my gran got sick and her parents adopted my father. According to family myth, this was so that his father would have no rights to him if my gran were to die. As it turned out, my gran didn't die and continued to live into her eighties, and my father got her surname, Shand, and my son got half his first name, Peter. So my dad was brought up in the home of his grandparents. Gran used to buy and sell houses, and when he was older she thought nothing of taking Dad out of school for weeks at a time to paint for her. When my dad was in high school Granny married again, but that didn't last long. She was in and out of relationships and got engaged several times. According to family legend, she was very popular with men. Meanwhile my father matriculated at the age of fifteen and then, because no one could think what to do with him and he was too young to go to UCT, Granny sent him back to school to redo his matric. The second time around he scored 100 per cent for maths.

When my father spoke it wasn't to make small talk; it was because he had something to say. Dad was a man of routine, a qualified chartered accountant who spent his life trying to escape the life-sucking monotony of office work. He was a decent man, a good provider and a hard worker. He looked out for us and he looked after us – his four motley children. Dad was a bit subversive, with little regard for bureaucracy, and thought nothing of signing official forms on our behalf. He was also very creative with our tax returns. He refused to pay our school fees because he paid his taxes – much to my embarrassment. But at the same time he was very civic-minded. He knew his rights but also his responsibilities. He once stood for Cape Town's City Council. Dad didn't let the system get him down and chose rather to rise above it. He was a real socialist at heart – and equally comfortable with McGregor's toothless, thumb-less, alcoholic mayor as he was with knighted guests staying at his guest house. He was a rebel and a gypsy but also an accountant and a responsible citizen.

My dad was particularly fond of Boy and spent a lot of time with him during his first four years, when we lived in McGregor. Any event that was taking place that he thought a boy would be interested in, he would fetch JP in his bakkie and take him along. My dad was like a rock, consistent, reliable and present – whether it was making endless trips to and from Grahamstown when I couldn't make up my mind whether I was leaving Rhodes or staying, or signing me up for free Old Mutual shares, or making sure I collected my UIF, or sitting on the management committee of the Waldorf school my children attended. My mother says that every night, in appreciation of her good cooking, he laid the table and lit the candles before the family sat down to eat supper. He was diagnosed with liver cancer at the age of seventy-two and died four weeks later. He refused a CAT scan (too expensive) and any further treatment after the initial diagnosis. He somehow knew how sick he was and he let go of life easily. Nursing him over those few days at the end were some of the most profound days of my life... until Boy died, that is. My father had a particular way of moving his hands, usually while working out some problem in his head. JP moved his hands in a way that reminded me of my father.

My Afrikaans-speaking mother, Helaine Potgieter, married my dad, an English-speaking South African, when she was just twenty years old. Added to the Afrikaans/English mix was a sixteen-year age gap. And even more scandalous, he was divorced with two sons, Andrew and Hamish, my half-brothers. Andrew was about nine and Hamish about five at the time they got married. Nina and I followed with only fifteen months between us.

Mom grew up in the Free State – Winburg and Bloemfontein – and in Bellville in the Western Cape. She was the oldest of three children, and at the end of her first year at UCT, where she was studying to be a drama teacher, her father died. She had to enter the workplace, and after a few junior journalist positions she applied for a job at Ninham Shand and Partners. Dad interviewed her. She left the interview and found her friend who was waiting for her in the foyer. Mom's first words to her were, 'I have just met the man I'm going to marry'. And a few months later she did. Before that, while they were still courting, Dad drove a red Alpha Spider and Mom says he always had a picnic blanket and a bottle of champagne in the boot.

Elise Coetzee, my grandmother on my mother's side, babysat for Boy the night before she died. He was about one and a half. She had lung cancer. She loved her brandy and smoked too many cigarettes. She created beautiful mosaics and gardens and was impatient with impractical people. She herself was incredibly practical, efficient and highly creative. Ouma loved and was fascinated by nature – especially birds. She grew up during the Depression on a farm near Cradock and was a real tomboy. Her husband, Dirk Potgieter (John Peter's great-grandfather), was the youngest of six children – a laatlammetjie. Ouma used to say that Dirk came from a family of poor farmers and that he had to walk barefoot to school from the farm, but as a cousin of my mom's points out, the family always had servants and smart Sunday clothes. Mom says Dirk grew up in a tough environment and that his father was hard and strict, having survived the Boer War.

Mom says her father was very loving and kind, 'always obliging and ready to give a helping hand'. Others said of Dirk that he was, above all else, a humble man. He could be relied on for his honesty and deep integrity. 'He sneaked off to church now and then', according to Mom. She also remembers:

> The other side of him was fun-loving, eating and drinking and laughing. I loved dancing with him – he was light as a feather on his feet and he had a beautiful singing voice and could belt out various opera arias. He was artistic and made beautiful things. He had a heart attack when he was thirty-four and his health became more and more debilitated...

Dirk died in his early forties of heart disease. Had he lived a few years longer, he could have had a bypass and lived a long and happy life.

David is one of five children – he was number four in four years. His father was a medical doctor and his mother worked as a secretary. Like JP, David was also a child who made few demands – even telling his mother each year that he didn't want a birthday party because he felt they couldn't afford it. Although he never had birthday parties as a child, he made up for that later by throwing some of the best and wildest parties in Cape Town as a young adult.

David's grandfather on his mother's side came out on a ship from Scotland as a twenty-year-old and worked his way up to be mayor of Knysna and a hotelier. By all accounts he was a strict

Scotsman with a great zest for life. He must have been a powerful force because I have been told many stories about him, but I can't remember any stories being told to me about his wife. He lived to the age of ninety-eight. He loved travelling, was exceptionally well dressed, loved good food and wine, walked and swam every day. He was disciplined but knew how to enjoy life. David's mother, Anne, married the young and dashing new doctor in town. David's father, Basil, was a reserved, dignified, well-known and highly respected man in Cape Town. He loved rugby and was a gifted player. He played wing for Western Province and almost became a Springbok except for some controversy that prevented him from getting there. He worked as a state doctor until he finally retired at eighty-five. I'm sure rearing five children on a state doctor's salary was a challenge. After Boy died, a story emerged that many years ago a very distant cousin in Scotland had killed himself at the age of seventeen, and that's the only suicide we know of on both sides of the family.

It was certainly a colourful and unusual family – going back generations – that John Peter was born into. What of it did he carry into his life? What did he inherit? The characteristics of humility, humour, reserve, creativity, integrity, reliability, eccentricity, a love of nature and great dress sense were certainly shared by Boy. But what in Boy's incarnation was his own and had nothing to do with the rest of us and the ghosts of family members now departed? And what of the scripts that David and I brought to the family we created and that John Peter grew up in?

15

I was born on 12 November 1968 in Cape Town and lived there until the age of nine, when my parents emigrated to Ireland, taking along my younger sister, my two older half-brothers, my granny and me. For five years we lived a semi-nomadic existence, moving many times as my parents worked in various places – a guest house, a vegetable garden, a pub, a restaurant, a castle and even a strawberry field. It was a rich, evocative experience for all of us.

We lived in an old cavernous mill that had been converted into a pub and accommodation. This was our first real home in Ireland. The pub was in a village with the unenviable distinction of being known as Ireland's dirtiest town. I loved living there. The old mill had so many rooms and so many floors. My sister and I shared a bedroom on the third floor and it felt like we were living on top of the world. It was a village of tinkers (Ireland's settled travelling people), a ruin of a Norse castle, an ancient graveyard, a butcher, a baker, a postmaster, a doctor, a priest, a Catholic church and a Protestant church. A carnival and horse gymkhanas and circuses came to town. The village and surrounding countryside were our playground, and every day was an adventure. We picked strawberries for pocket money and rode horses or our bicycles, heading along meandering lanes until we stopped for a picnic. We had such freedom! We could choose our route without an adult in sight, making our own way across fields of cows and sheep, avoiding the odd bull when picking blackberries from the hedgerows when we got hungry. We'd come home in the evening dirty and tired.

My parents worked long, hard hours first running the pub, and then they started a restaurant in the basement of an old guest house. We moved to a tiny cottage at a crossroads in the middle of the Irish countryside. My sister and I slept in the attic, which we had insulated with old newspaper, my parents' double bed just fitted in the downstairs bedroom and Granny's bedroom was a caravan outside. Every morning we came down the ladder – it couldn't really be called a staircase – into the warm cosy kitchen, where we ate a hot breakfast before our half-hour walk to catch the bus to the Protestant school in Wexford. During those long winter months it was dark when we got up and by the time we got home in the afternoon. There would be a fire burning in the small lounge, and when she wasn't working in the restaurant, my mother would have picked something from the hedgerows or veggie garden and transformed it into a hearty and nurturing supper. I remember they made wine from elderberries, strawberries, blackberries and, I suppose, whatever else would ferment. My mother is a gifted cook and could make rabbit and guinea fowl tasty.

In the summer months when I got home from school, I immediately pulled on my jodhpurs and boots and went off to the stables. I would walk, skip or run down narrow lanes with hedgerows on either side full of juicy blackberries, being careful not to get stung by nettles. Or I would follow bridle paths snaking their way up, across and down embankments – magical paths that took me on journeys deep into my fertile imagination full of strange musings and yearnings. In summer the land was very green and soft, but in winter when it snowed or there was frost on the ground the earth became brittle and crunchy underfoot. The stables were very old. You entered through high gates that opened into a cobbled circular yard surrounded by individual stables. To the left stood an ancient stone used as a mounting block, and to the right was the blacksmith's forge. The blacksmith would come once a month to shoe the horses. I remember the blazing orange-yellow-white flames, the bellows whooshing, the sharp clip-clang of metal on metal. Next to the forge was the tack room, where I spent many hours polishing and dubbining saddles and bridles. I can still smell the wet leather and the polish.

We also lived in rooms in a castle in the west of Ireland on the edge of the largest private-owned lake in Europe. The owners didn't live there and my parents were hired as the managers of the estate. My sister and I had bedrooms in the basement of the castle, and the castle and its grounds were our playground during the school holidays.

Just before we left Ireland, we lived in a half-renovated house in the countryside a couple of miles' walk from the nearest village. My father was working in the nearby town, and my mother and Granny were tending an acre of strawberries that were harvested in summer and sold to a nearby co-op.

In between the many adventures were long periods of boredom. We often lived in isolated places far from friends, and as I got older and moved into my teenage years it did get lonely with just my younger sister and me home from boarding school for holidays. Fortunately I was an avid reader and would get lost in novels for days. Or I would go for long walks on my own, full of a deep longing and an impossible imagination, wishing with all my heart to find the love of my life – probably not in person, just the idea of love itself that I read about in the endless novels I consumed so voraciously.

My most vivid memories of Ireland are of children. Everyone seemed to come from a large family. Children were loved. I remember the tinker women selling roasted chestnuts on Dublin's Grafton Road. Their old-fashioned large-wheeled prams were overflowing with babies with pale faces, snotty noses and red hair. Homes were warm and loving and chaotic, smelling of urine and damp. Beds had nylon sheets that never seemed to get completely dry. Some of the children of these houses used to sleep four to a double bed. In some homes I couldn't quite work out how many children there were. My oldest brother dated a girl from a family of twenty-one children. Granny was horrified. I loved it all. The Catholic church also fills my memory. Strange rituals involving the Virgin Mary, candles, incense, white dresses for First Communion, crosses made from palm fronds, ash on foreheads, wafers and wine. I so wanted to join my friends for Holy Communion. I didn't understand any of it except they were allowed to go up to the altar and for some reason I wasn't. The confession box held an equal if not greater allure. How I longed to enter that small space and confess my sins. It was all so secretive and my friends seemed so important standing in line to do this special thing that would purify and release.

I remember my last ever horse-riding lesson – days before leaving Ireland for South Africa. I am riding a large strong chestnut and I am jumping barrels – and higher – and I am doing very well. My instructor is working me hard and won't take 'No, I can't' for an answer. I don't want him to see how scared I've become. I know I am doing well, and it's exhilarating. I have never ridden like this before, but I am shaking inside. I have lost my nerve – too many falls, I suppose – and I have realised that riding is dangerous. I am fourteen, and it's the last time I ride like this.

John O'Donohue writes beautifully about Ireland's ancient Celtic and pagan landscape (and one of my many lifelines has been his exquisite poem 'A Blessing for the Family and Friends of a Suicide'). His poetry is imbued with the Ireland of my childhood and early adolescence. He writes about boundaries and the stone walls of Ireland that demarcate tiny pieces of land – yet these walls are full of openings and apertures, allowing rabbits and hares to move freely between the fields and ferns, nettles and briars to grow on and through the layers of ancient stone. These are walls that demarcate spaces but don't limit and shut out life. Walls that are porous, walls that breathe.

John Peter had built a solid wall around him and imprisoned himself in there. Over the years he'd built the bricks up one by one until he couldn't even see over the top. With each hurt and unkindness, real or imagined, another brick was added, but it wasn't a soft cocoon he nestled into – it was hard, cold stone. He made sure it was secure enough that nothing could penetrate. The moment he put that tie around his neck, whatever small openings were left had closed. In that moment nothing could get through. We left Ireland when I was fourteen – the age JP was when he died. Moving from Ireland back to South Africa was a threshold moment for me and I remember it very well. From a small, elite and gentle boarding school in Ireland I went to Bryanston High – a huge ugly government edifice – in Johannesburg. I remember the barren playing fields of yellow grass burning under the relentless sun. Everything was dry and faded by the sun, and everything was big. The sky was big. The school was big. The landscape was big. The houses and cars were big. And the teachers were so foreign. They hardly knew who was in their class and seemed to care less. All they were concerned about was hair and nails and the length of your school skirt. We had to stand in queues – queues for everything – and march on the field like soldiers. I could hardly comprehend what was going on. Was this school? We were just numbers – there was no room for individuality. I fought against it. My rebellious spirit found expression fighting against being a nameless girl standing in a line. And at that age, what are more evocative symbols of rebellion than hair and clothes? I re-invented myself and started experimenting, wanting to be the most outrageous and different fourteen-year-old around. I had to assert my individuality in order to survive the perceived prison I found myself in.

I know John Peter would have loved the freedom of a rural Irish childhood. A childhood where each day is an adventure. I moved from my cocooned middle-class life in Cape Town into a strange, exciting and foreign country. A new country where the signposts had to be re-navigated. For so many years we moved, changed schools, lived in unusual homes that changed from year to year. With each move we were the new kids, the foreign kids, the special kids. I was different. I had a different history, a different geography, culture and accent. With each move the story of my life was rewritten all over again. Sometimes I could completely erase a particular part of my past, and sometimes it was a partial rewrite, and the layers of stories that have become my biography were built up like a palimpsest. In Ireland I was the child from Africa and back in South Africa I was the teenager from Ireland. How much of this history formed and moulded my identity as an adult and parent? I had itchy feet, as well as expectations I could probably never meet, and I longed not to settle into a conventional middle-class life. And I keenly felt a sense of difference and never quite belonging and fitting in anywhere. What of this geographic and emotional landscape did John Peter inherit?

16

McGregor is my soul home and it probably represented the same to John Peter: a place where we both have felt safe and at home. I was twenty-one years old and in my final year at Rhodes University when my parents bought the Old Mill. The name had a resonance, as they had bought the Old Mill Inn in Ireland many years previously. Arriving in McGregor, I remember driving up the gravel road and into an oasis. The large majestic oak tree in the parking area looked as though it had been there forever. Sprinklers irrigated the green grass pathway that led up to a Georgian house nestled among jacaranda and syringa trees, with their purple and yellow petals forming a carpet on the ground. There was a vivid cerise bougainvillea and honeysuckle and jasmine blossoms. A stone path meandered through a rose garden up to the main homestead: a long whitewashed thatched house with a stoep overlooking the village and a vineyard. Shiny Oregon wood floors and yellowwood ceilings graced the main house – there was a dining room, a kitchen, the reception area and a guest lounge. Outside stood an ancient mill, and on the other side of the property were eight guest rooms also under thatch. I fell in love with the Old Mill immediately. It was as though I'd always known that this place existed and it had just been waiting for me to find it one day.

My parents and Granny camped out on the bottom floor of the

Georgian house, which was actually an old converted barn. There were two en suite bedrooms and a small lounge. That was their 'private' space. Upstairs were three small loft rooms under a very low ceiling, and that's where family members stayed when we came to visit. I knew the moment the car drove up the driveway that one day I would live there and help run the Old Mill. When David and I were newly married, we bought olive trees and planted a grove next to the swimming pool as our commitment to return one day.

I married David when I was twenty-two years old – or should that be twenty-two years young? Like my mother and her mother and I'm sure her mother before her, I was a young bride. I was so innocent and romantic, with a head full of strange ideas and yearnings. To be honest, I married largely because I didn't really know what else to do with my life. I had no vision, no plan, no list of places I wanted see, jobs I wanted to do, careers I wanted to pursue. I had a BA in journalism and English from Rhodes, and I had spent a year in McGregor helping my parents run their guest house in between abortive trips back to Grahamstown, first to start an honours degree and then to work at the Rhodes library, but actually I just wanted to be close to the man I had fallen in love with there. I really was a bit of a mess. Not long before, I had been involved in a very destructive relationship that ended after I started cutting my arms and got such a fright that I packed up in the middle of the night and did a duck.

So that's what David got – a decidedly off-centre, paranoid, directionless, messed-up wife. I got a heavy-drinking freelance actor who wanted to have a good time. Perhaps this was not an ideal foundation upon which to start a marriage or a family. But before I knew it I was pregnant with Laine, and only then did I realise I was going to have to work to earn a living. Our cash flow was extremely erratic – it was either feast or famine, and with a little one on the way, famine had lost its appeal. After Laine was born, we moved into a house in Berea near the Johannesburg city centre, and then Annie came along, followed by John Peter. There I was, twenty-seven years old with three children aged four and under, running my own little writing/editing/research business from home, knowing I would have to get a full-time job to keep the show on the road and not wanting to leave my babies. In short, I was feeling quite vulnerable.

My solution – back then I always had a solution, or at least was always able to make some sort of decision – was to move David, the kids and me to McGregor, where I could help my parents run the guest house. I'm not sure David had any real say in the matter. I put our Berea house on the market and luckily it sold quickly. So we packed up and by December 1996 we were on our way to McGregor – with, I must admit, no real plan in place. As it was, my parents inherited this rather alternative young family – I suppose I sort of handed over responsibility. I was there, I was willing to work long hard hours, and in exchange they had to look after us. And they did. We moved into a cottage they owned in the village and for our labour we got accommodation, food, domestic help, school fees and tips for pocket money. The rest of our expenses were up to us. Not surprisingly, David couldn't earn money as an actor in McGregor and in a relatively short period of time our relationship spiralled downwards into a quagmire we couldn't find our way out of – but I'll come back to that.

Our cottage was very romantic. It was over 100 years old and had wooden floors and high wooden ceilings with wooden shutters on the front windows. There was an outside staircase up to the loft. We had two bedrooms – one for David and me and the other for the three little ones. There was a kitchen and a living room and a bathroom, as well as a little room off the stoep. The kitchen door opened onto a rambling back garden. Nina, her husband and Sarah, their baby daughter, lived in the converted shed next door. My father built John Peter a large tree house in the old peppercorn tree in the back garden. A leiwatersloot ran in front of the house and Boy grew up in that sloot, splashing and playing in the running water.

As a baby and toddler, John Peter was so easy. He used to fit in effortlessly and just go along with whatever was happening. As my mother used to say, '*Hy gaan maar ook saam.*' He had a slightly oriental look and with his dark deep eyes he reminded me of a blond version of a Tibetan child. He didn't talk until he was three. Perhaps in some families this would have been taken as a sign that something was 'wrong', but we simply accepted him as he presented himself. He spoke when he was ready, when he needed to.

Boy could swim from the age of two – I remember him amazing the guests at Warmwaterberg with his underwater swimming ability at that young age. He loved to swim and to be in water. But he swam like a natural creature does, as just something he did and enjoyed – not for him the competition of racing or swimming lengths for exercise. My mother remembers:

> I think partly why I want to go there [Warmbaths in Barrydale] is because John Peter was always so happy there. I've got a photograph of a time when Peter and I took your three children there on our own. He was still very small. I remember how he attracted the attention of everyone by jumping into the cold pools [in the middle of winter] after he got all red and hot in the warm water. And then back into the warm water he went when he was blue with cold. He was completely into this game and everyone laughed and enjoyed his fun with him. When we came past there from Calitzdorp last July, he asked longingly, 'When can we go again?' …

There were always enough arms for my young Boy. There was a kitchen full of women at my parents' guest house: Sophie, our Parisian au pair; Kettie, our domestic worker; my mother; my sister; his sisters. Everyone wanted to pick up and hold Boy. He was chubby, blond, black-eyed, serious and easy-going – even weaning him was easy. Everyone loved him.

When Boy was a toddler I noticed pus and blood on his pillow one morning and I saw that a discharge was dripping from his ear. His eardrum had perforated and he didn't make a murmur. I took him to Keith, a retired ear-and-throat doctor then living in McGregor. He said no antibiotics were needed and no grommets either. He explained that Boy's eardrum had made its own grommet and was draining just fine. Stopyn is all he prescribed to help dry up the discharge and for pain relief. And so for years that's what we did with Boy until he grew out of his ear infections. I'm not even sure when that was – for years Boy had ear infections, and then one day they were gone. I often wonder if those ear infections should have been treated differently. Perhaps having his ears plugged up with all that pus and goo meant he couldn't hear very well. Maybe that is why he only started talking when he was three.

It was also when Boy was three that David and I divorced. David went back to living in Johannesburg and stopped drinking, and I found myself in the middle of a wild love affair. I have a memory of John Peter's third birthday. He got a beautiful train set, but he didn't get excited about it. I put it together for him and he went through the motions of playing with it but with no enthusiasm. His flatness struck me then. Looking back, I wonder if he was depressed. At the time I wondered if he had always been like this and I had simply not noticed. Was he feeling down because his father was absent? Or was I merely projecting and he was actually behaving like any little boy who would far rather be outside playing in the *leiwater* and digging in the mud and climbing trees and playing with toktokkie?

After we got divorced, John Peter went on a road trip with David, who was off to do a one-man show in Mossel Bay and Plettenberg Bay. David remembers:

> I had a strange experience with Boy when he was little. I fetched him from McGregor and we drove to Mossel Bay and found the farmhouse where we were staying for the night. The farmer was there, along with his wife and two young children. The farmer had been a boarder at Rondebosch Boys so, although he was younger than me, I got on with him and we had lots to share and talk about. They had a guest house going on the farm. I unpacked our bags and we went down to the beach and there was a tidal pool and Boy wanted to swim. It was too cold for me to swim as the sun was setting, but I let him swim in the tidal pool. We then went back and had supper with the family. The next day there were lots

of farm things to do. The farmer had a two-litre Coke bottle with a teat on it to feed a baby lamb in a pen. And when the old black man came to feed the lamb, we were watching and he gave Boy the Coke bottle so he could feed the lamb. I remember how shocked he was at how strongly the lamb sucked at the teat. We spent hours watching the farm help load up cattle onto trucks.

I had a show that night and I put Boy to bed first and only left once he was asleep. The farmer's wife kept an eye on him. I did the show and the next day we packed up and drove to Plett. I had arranged a babysitter for Plett because the house we were staying in was a stand-alone and nobody lived there. We arrived in Plett and I unpacked my props and set everything up and did the technical stuff and JP just sat on a chair and watched.

After setting everything up we went to Keurboom and again he wanted to swim and he ran and played in the waves. I remember taking him back to the house and getting him ready for bed before the babysitter arrived. I asked him if he wanted to shower and he did and I put him into the shower. Suddenly he just started crying violently – he was absolutely terrified. It was like real fear. I didn't understand it because he had showered before. It was like he was standing there and he was in complete fear and he was crying uncontrollably and he said, 'I'm scared'. I said, 'It's fine, you don't have to shower.' He didn't get out, he just stood there, and there was this strange fear, almost primal. It stayed with me because it was such a strange reaction. He was really, really terrified. I couldn't understand it. It made no sense.

I dressed him and then the babysitter came and I went across and did the show and everything was fine.

The next morning I dressed him in his sailor outfit – the one your mom made for him – and took some photos of him outside the theatre. We then went across to Knysna for his cousin's christening. We had to leave early because we had to drive back. Most of the time we were driving he would fall asleep. He would just sit there because he was too short to see out the window. He would sit and then fall asleep and he would lie with his head in the corner of the seat and just be asleep. At that stage he hardly spoke. He'd want to do things like go to the beach and swim, but he'd get in the car when it was time to leave. He just went along, that is how he was. And so we drove back. When we arrived back home, I think he was still in his sailor suit, and quite dirty from all the cakes we ate after the christening.

17

So yes, I was young and I was wild, but I loved those three little ones with all my heart, and where I could not provide stability I was certain my parents picked up the slack. It takes a village to raise a child, as the saying goes, and my children were in the best village and leading very healthy and expansive little lives. But is love enough? A year after David and I divorced, I took the children to the Grahamstown National Arts Festival to see their father and I asked him if I could come back. He said yes. So a couple of months later the house was packed up and I was making the long drive to Johannesburg. Laine stayed behind with my parents to finish Grade 2 and Annie and JP came up with me.

Our reunion lasted just over a year. During that time we moved from a rented house in Westdene to a large ungainly Art Deco house in Greenside. It may have been plain and odd from the outside, but inside the house had wooden floors and high ceilings, Art Deco detail, and lots of rooms. David and I spent months taking out carpets and sanding and varnishing floors. But without couples' counselling to sort out why we ended up such a muddle in the first place, old patterns of behaviour re-emerged, and eventually I moved out of our house and into a garden cottage down the road. John Peter had nearly finished his last year at nursery school. David and I shared custody of the children – one week on and one week off.

David told me a very sad story after Boy died. He had gone into his bedroom and JP, who was six or seven, was lying on the double bed. He looked so sad lying there staring at the ceiling. David asked him, 'What are you thinking about, Boy?' and he said, 'I miss my mother'.

That year – 2003 – was a dark period of shattered self and my self-esteem was at an all-time low. I think I was quite desperate really, perhaps having a breakdown of sorts but still holding it together – just. One evening after I had put the children to bed, I opened a bottle of wine and started drinking and painting – it was a self-portrait – and the more I drank the crazier I became and the more violent the painting. I felt an irresistible urge to paint with my own blood and so I cut my arms and let the blood drip onto the portrait and mingled it with the paint and then wrote 'guilty as charged'. On the painting I pasted photos of my children at birth. It was the mingling of my image with the paint, with the blood, with the photos of their birth from my bloody loins... an external representation of all my love, all my pain, and all my guilt at not being the perfect mother, of being a mother who had failed. Failed to keep my marriage together. And in the morning I got up and with sore bloody arms got the children ready for school and they asked me what happened and I said I fell into the bougainvillea bush and it scratched my arms. Did I really think they would believe me?

A couple of months before John Peter died he said to me, 'What sort of mother are you?' I was taken aback, but as I've spent decades pondering the same question I didn't mind. In fact, coming from Boy I felt it was healthy and good to ask the question. My immediate thought was *He's expressing himself, he's angry, he's asking and this is good*. He made reference to my shaven head from university days. And then he said, 'What sort of mother cuts her arms and paints her picture with the blood?' He was only seven years old, but he knew exactly what I'd done despite my pathetic attempt to hide it.

That was a bad year for me and it was John Peter's seventh year. According to Rudolf Steiner, that age is a period when the inner forces of a young child are working to transform the body from one that was inherited from the parents to one that represents the full personality of the child. And Boy had a very confused, chaotic and spirited mother. I want to write that on the surface I still seemed to be coping with the children and work and so on. But perhaps even on the surface cracks were appearing. Definitely beneath the surface I was entering a dark and desperate place. I felt so bad about myself. David's anger towards me – which was no doubt justified – didn't help. By the time the year was up, I was ready to go back to David and return to some semblance of normality, order and routine, and maybe just to have him stop hating me. It couldn't have helped Boy to have a mother like me during his first year of primary school. I was as painfully self-conscious of all my shortcomings, imagined or otherwise, as he was of his. He was very shy, but nevertheless he had friends and play dates and went to birthday parties. And his teacher remembers him fondly. He was a quiet boy, but he was present.

And so David and I made the decision to reconcile – again. I wanted to provide my children with stability and two parents under one roof. And I knew I wanted to have a fourth child. I had always known I would have four children. So I became pregnant and we remarried – in a church this time and slightly sheepishly, as who on earth was going to take us seriously after the past couple of years? Only a few close friends and family were invited, and it turned out to be a beautiful day. John Peter carried the ring, Laine and Annie were flower girls, and it was all perfect. When I look at the wedding video now for footage of John Peter, it's amazing how in the background he was. The girls are everywhere, all over the video, but John Peter hardly features.

In any event, life got back to normal – or at least our version of normal.

18

Almost immediately after Boy's death, we begin a kind of forensic investigation, searching for the answer to the one question that nearly drove us mad: *Why?* We start looking for hints, for clues – any 'evidence' for why he did what he did – the day after he died. My mother is the most able and thorough investigator, especially at the beginning, when I am incapable of doing much more than lie on the couch and cry. She goes to his room and finds his rucksack all neatly packed with intention. He had rolled up an orange blanket and a sleeping bag and tied them both firmly with rope to the outside of the rucksack. Inside he had packed a packet of rice, a couple of tins of baked beans, a cooking pot, a collection of nails, some rope and his bicycle repair kit. He had even stitched the eagle from his belt buckle onto the front of the rucksack. He was ready to go. My mother searches his clothes and finds a list in the pocket of the black jacket Ruby had slept in the night after he died. The list, as Boy wrote it, is as follows:

Hunting knife (NB)
Pellet gun
Duct tape
First aid kit
Water purryifyer system (NB)

Fire starting things
Rope
Vegetable seeds

The list is written with different pens as though he started the list and then went back to it later to add the NBs and the rope and the vegetable seeds. He had been planning to run away. Is that why he stole the money? He was going to run away to the wild and live a self-sustainable life. He was going to build a shelter, make fires to cook, get water from the river and purify it with his pills, plant seeds for food, hunt small animals to eat. He was going to get there on his bicycle.

David's therapist told him that we would have gone mad if Boy had run away and we never found him. I don't know about that – at least then there would have been a chance he is still alive. As I write this, I know that I cannot begin to imagine what it must be like to search and not find a child. But we all choose to read the runaway pack as a poignant 'letter', as his farewell note to us. It tells us that he didn't want to be here anymore. He had to get away and not just from us, but from everyone. He wanted to be in a different place, where the pressure was less and all he had to focus on was his survival and not algebra or comprehension or history projects. It was a metaphor for the journey he did end up taking away from it all, from this life that was just too difficult for him.

I go through his school books one by one, scouring the pages for anything that might explain why he did what he did, but all I see is a child who had clearly lost interest in the experiment called school. His homework diary had one entry in it. His handwriting was scratchy and light and non-committal, so unlike the letters and numbers he formed so neatly and carefully when he was younger. I feel so dreadful, so absolutely inadequate, as though I had neglected him. Why did I not see this complete lack of interest in school? Why did I not ask to see his books? Why did I not pay more attention to his schoolwork and his homework? But I suppose I was never a mother who involved herself too much in her children's school life or assignments other than to help with homework when it was really necessary or when the children asked for my help. It's how my mother treated me. School and homework were my problem and responsibility. But then I was a different child, one who wanted to do well and to excel.

I have learned in this hunt for clues and missed messages that I can lose myself in the self-recrimination and blame and guilt if I choose to. But then, like a lifeline, other memories come in. I remember how I bunked work one day and didn't take the three of them to school. Instead we packed some sandwiches and spent the morning on a little rowing boat on Zoo Lake and we laughed and we connected and we were happy. A few weeks before his death, before the end of term one, I somehow found out JP had been assigned a history project. It was like pulling teeth but I sat and helped him, and he wrote his project out neatly and decorated the cover and showed interest. It looked very good and I knew he would get a nice mark for it and thought maybe he would feel good about that. But he hanged himself before he got the mark.

Annie is the one who eventually finds a page neatly glued down in one of his Grade 8 exercise books. They are the only words of his we have that reveal anything about his interior life:

> 20 January 2010
> What if I were to run away from everyone and everything. My whole life sucks. Everyone hates me. They are all fuck ups. Why am I hated by everyone. If only I could die I wouldn't have to see any of these motherfuckers ever again no one ever. That would make my life the best seeing no-one I know ever again. These bitches I am going to run away I fucking swear.

Just a handful of sentences written at the start of Grade 8 – and before he started smoking dagga. (His sisters told me that JP started smoking dagga in the June holidays of that year.) He writes them and he glues down the page onto the hard cover of the exercise book in order to hide what he has written. Did what he wrote scare him? Was the intensity of his anger and feelings overwhelming? He didn't tear the page out and crumple up what he had written and throw it away. He kept it and neatly glued it down so that the words still existed but no one would see them and only he knew they were there.

A year and a half after his death, I speak to Fikile about John Peter. Fikile has lived with us and worked for us since Boy was six years old. She is part of our family, a second mother to my children. In those early months after John Peter died, Fikile would be waiting for me in her running shoes when I got back from work. She would say to me, 'Come, we're going for a walk.' Every evening we would go for a brisk walk, and sometimes a run, around Greenside. We would walk or run in silence. If we spoke it would be about JP. When my mind can't conjure up a shopping list or come up with a meal for supper or even remember that supper has to be made, Fikile is there. She makes the shopping lists, she plans the meals, she cooks them. She plants spinach and basil. She shows me the shoots. She harvests the plants. She gently tries to keep me interested in the wonder of my garden. She isn't a psychologist, but she knows that exercise and new growth in the garden can keep the spirit from atrophying.

I tell her I am writing a book about John Peter. I ask her if there is anything she wants to share with me, anything she has remembered that she hasn't shared with me yet. And she tells me that every day of the week before he died he'd say to her, 'Fikile, I'm going away'. And Fikile said she'd laugh and ask, 'Where are you going to go, JP?' and he'd repeat, 'I'm going away'. He told her, 'That hobo who comes to the gate and asks for food and old clothes – I'm going to speak to him and find out how he lives, and I'm going away like him. And when I am hungry I will come back to the house and you will give me food.' And Fikile said, 'No, JP, I won't give you food.' And Boy just laughed and said, 'Yes, you will.'

She tells me that in December before he died he was looking in the deep freeze and he turned to her and asked, 'Did you fail your driver's licence again?' and Fikile said, 'Yes, I did, JP'. And he asked her, 'Why don't you kill yourself?' And Fikile laughed again and said, 'Why would I do that, JP? I am going to go and try again when I turn fifty.'

She tells me that every day of the week before he died he'd say to her, 'Fikile, I'm not going back to that school next term.'

She tells me that he told her, 'My mom is disappointed with my school report.'

She tells me that he would come home from school and show her photos he'd taken of the boys fighting at school. He would say to her, 'I don't like the fighting.'

My mother remembers:

> My darling child, I have been trying to pluck up the courage to phone you but feel too brittle, sad and tearful to talk. It felt very good to plant the aloe at his grave on his birthday. John Peter, I know, approves. I have been with you and David and the girls in spirit the whole day. But most of all my mind wanders to that boy, to the dreadfulness of it all. I want to feel grateful that at least we did have him for those fourteen years and we did know the gentleness of his spirit and how he tried so hard to be a toughie, a real boy. I sat on the bed crying with *Hector the Helicopter* in my hands. I must have read it a million times. He asked for it over and over. About a sea rescue and braveness. And so we carry on… with our own braveness and rescue. We will hold each other tightly. Sleep well. All my love as always.

And so even as a little boy he was trying to be a toughie – but he just wasn't.

A friend of my mother's who lives in McGregor wrote to her after Boy died:

> My dearest girl Helaine,
>
> I am doing this in this way because I promised my son that I would, and I have just put the telephone down after talking to him. He will be forty in September … my youngest. He asked me to give you his love. But the important thing is that he told me that at school he had a friend of John Peter's age who did the same thing. He wanted me to tell you that *nobody*, but *nobody*, could have altered John Peter's intention. He said that he had often talked to

the boy he knew, and that his friend was simply overcome with 'being alive in this world', and that with all the happenings in the world the friend did not want to be a part of this world any longer. My son said that he could understand that. At fourteen, with all the emotional turmoil that age brings, this lad, Marc, just did not want to handle it. Nothing and nobody could have changed his mind. My son also said that as one sees the world today, it seems so much worse anyway than it was then, and later, my son asked friends of his partner, Marlene, who is a wonderful Welsh lady and a doctor, and they have said that there are some people who are born with a genetic tendency to do this, and the most vulnerable age is the fourteen-to-sixteen age group. Even more so today than when he went through it with Marc.

More words from my mother:

I have also just thought how, in the last year of his life, I spent about three months with him. I 'detected' nothing of what was to come. Always so good to have him around!!!

Nina says when she thinks of John Peter it is always the baby/toddler that she remembers. She says when he stayed here over the years she just saw him and that was it. No real contact. But the little one touched her deeply – so quiet. Was he depressed already?

19

There is a tightening in my chest, a feeling of dread. It's as if I've had a glimpse of what was happening and what could have been. I had clicked on a link to the video *Henry's Story*, twenty-eight minutes long. Henry started experimenting with dagga when he was fourteen years old. He moved from dagga to hallucinogens and party drugs and from there to prescription pills, and at the end had started using heroin. By the time he was eighteen he was dead from an overdose, and he had also been badly beaten.

In the video Henry's family talk about what happened to him. Words and phrases jump out – echoes of my own experience with my son: *he was shy... he was different... it was like when he started smoking dagga a switch went on... he told his mom when he started smoking dagga he had an a-ha moment: 'so this is what I'm supposed to feel like' ... he was aware then that it had triggered something in him that he wasn't able to switch off... he was a kid like any other... he started smoking dagga when he was fourteen years old... it was sort of like a slow drip-drip-drip and I couldn't get a handle on what was going on... of course we all thought he'd grow up like the rest of us and go to college and have girlfriends... it wasn't supposed to end like this... it seemed like he was just getting up to mischief and at the start it was not the problem it was to become... he was quieter, he was a little different... slowly it seems like all the things you are doing are going to stop it, and slowly it turns into a situation where you realise oh my goodness, not only did it not stop, it has escalated... I didn't understand what was going on... I did not know what to do... he saw counsellors... one counsellor said, 'I can't do anything for him. He seems like he is sad but there's nothing wrong with him.'* His mother said that towards the end of his life 'what we were looking at was Henry becoming a homeless person...'

We searched the home computer for Internet history searches. We got into his Facebook page. But we found nothing. Not even a hint of what was to come. Had he deleted everything? John Peter's cellphone was another of the places we searched for clues. We discovered he had a dealer (and according to the girls a lot of pornography, but I didn't look). I remember thinking, *Fuck! A dealer? Dealers are for drug addicts...* but where else would he get his dagga from? After he died, his dealer sent an SMS: 'got shrooms for you'. I assume the mushrooms were for AfrikaBurn. I had planned a trip to this Karoo festival for the holidays, mainly for John Peter's sake. I knew I had to get him out of the city, away from what was causing his agitation, discomfort, dis-ease – take him somewhere stark and beautiful and in nature.

But we didn't get there.

I remember watching the movie *Woodstock* (the enacted one) with Boy a few months before he died, and he was transfixed. He was watching the characters tripping on LSD, feeling the excitement of the event, the adrenalin, the freedom. For me it was just so good to be sitting next to him and watching a video together. I spoke to him then about LSD and how it can fry the brain and do permanent neurological damage. He just thought what he was watching was awesome. And it was, in a way...

In our case, how did the situation spiral out of control in such a short period of time? And as I take the route of the drug angle – for with JP there are many stories and roads to follow – I'm sure there are lots of people out there who would blame the dagga smoking for what happened to Boy. It's an easy hook. But if you look at his complete biography, his psychology, his spirituality, his creativity, there are many threads that weave together to tell his story. And even as I pick up the threads and try to unravel them and make sense of them, there are some that are invisibly woven into his tapestry, holding secrets and yearnings and mischief and I'm sure a sadness that none of us knew.

Another video I watched on YouTube is about Jamey Robemeyer who killed himself at the age of fourteen in September 2011 – a few months after JP died. I watched his parents being interviewed, I watched Jamey's video blogs, I watched Lady Gaga dedicate a concert to him, and I heard his father say, 'He fooled everyone and put on a brave face'. Jamey was articulate, outspoken, confident. On a video blog from May 2011, Jamey said, 'I just want to say it does get better. All you have to do is love yourself and you will be safe.' His blogging comes across as a sort of a diary and a confident, empowering act. But the messages left on his blog by peers are devastating in their cruelty, lack of tolerance and unkindness: 'Jamey is stupid, gay, fat and ugly and must die.' Comments like these continued after he died. Jamey's mother says the negative messages made him feel 'worthless'. The father says, 'Get your kids to talk. We tried to get Jamey to talk, but he wouldn't. He just put up a brave face.' Did John Peter's peers say unkind things to him? Was he hated? Did he feel hated? Was he bullied?

JP was his own person and he led his own life. And as much as I believed that because I had birthed him and nursed him and loved him, I therefore knew him – I didn't and I don't. Yes, he smoked dagga – too much, according to his sisters. But how much did he actually use, and for how long? Did this drug exaggerate and exacerbate what was already latent – the despair, the hopelessness, the lack of ambition and drive, the inability to connect, no belief in God (from a young age), an urge to run away, feelings of being hated and persecuted, thoughts of dying, of killing himself? I don't know, but my mother's instinct tells me that if JP hadn't killed himself that day he would have continued smoking dagga and he would have taken the 'shrooms' and he probably would have taken anything offered to him. Sometimes I think of him like that: a dealer or peer says, 'Here's some crack. It's really cool, try some.'

And he'd respond: 'Oh *ja*, crack – I'll try that.'

It's like the switch – the one Henry's aunt describes – had been turned on from birth. It's as if his brain was wired differently. He was not risk averse and perhaps he didn't have that part of him developed that is meant to protect you, meant to make you feel some fear or anxiety; he just didn't have it. If you don't really see the point of life, then what is to stop you from trying anything? And I sensed that in him in a way – that lack of enthusiasm for life. It was as if his life force was underdeveloped, and maybe smoking dagga diminished what little he had.

So much in those last few months is vivid and immediate to me. I remember telling him again and again what a perfect birth I'd had with him. I would describe it – I'd tell him how peaceful and beautiful and pain free it was – and how I hadn't expected a boy and I'd burst into tears when the midwife told me, 'It's a boy'. Although he didn't seem to respond, I told him over and over and over – as though if I told him enough times, he'd understand how important life was, how important his life was, and how important he was to me who gave life to him.

What was his future? In those early months after he died – when we were all still together and we spent time talking about our boy – we had a similar realisation: none of us had ever imagined Boy as an adult, married with kids, going to work every day. Do other parents imagine their sons all grown up? I can see my three girls clearly and vividly as adults taking their place in the world. I can imagine what work they could do – the men they may marry – I can see them mothering…

But as for John Peter, to this day I can't picture him grown up. I try, but I can't imagine him as an adult, and it hurts so deeply that I can't.

20

At the end of Grade 4, John Peter asked me if he could change schools. He said he didn't want to be at the nearby government primary school anymore. He started nagging me every day about changing schools, telling me at every possible moment that he didn't want to go back to his primary school. I kept asking him why, but he couldn't answer. He only said he didn't want to be there anymore. So eventually I said, 'Okay, I will find you another school, but please write me a letter explaining to me why and what has happened.' This is what he wrote to me:

Mom Please can you take to a new
School because people in my class are rude
tome because today We were watching
Shrek 2 and theres a part in the movie
and they said that I must Practise the
Part becuse I look like Sherk and they
said I was fat thats anourther reason
why I dont like my stupid stupid School
and I have to go to another School
because I am going to die if I
dont go to another School Please Please
Please Please Please Please Please or I
Wont talk to anyone forever and I
am not Joking OK so Please Please
Please Please Please Please Please Please

please please please please please please
please please please please please please
please please please please please please
please please please please please please
please please please please please please
please please please please please please
please please I am beging you with all
my heart and soul so please please please
please please please please please please
please please please please please
please please please please please
please please please please please
please please please please please
please please please please please
please please please please please
please please please please please

So I found a beautiful, gentle, alternative school for him, Anam Cara (Gaelic for 'soul friend'), where JP was enrolled for Grade 5. It was run by two esoteric and eccentric older women who provided a haven for children who don't fit into the mainstream. Boy was happy there that year, and I liked him being there. His eczema improved. His eyes brightened. His expression was more open. He was happier in himself. They are angels, those women. His school report from July 2007 gave an average mark of 80 per cent and included comments such as 'John Peter is such a treat – smart, funny and good-looking! ... His work is of a high standard, just needs a little more confidence in his maths abilities... I enjoy his imaginative work (written and verbal!) and am delighted he is in my class...' The September 2007 report noted: 'JP has an excellent brain, which can allow him to achieve excellent results, however he does not seem to be motivated to produce these results on his own. He needs a lot of encouragement to give of his best. Occasionally I am lucky enough to see a wonderful, mischievous young man with a great sense of humour – come on, JP, let him out more!'

After a full year at Anam Cara, I took JP and Annie for a complete psycho-educational assessment at the end of 2007. I think the time spent at Anam Cara was more a year of building self-esteem and confidence than doing schoolwork. After Boy died, I looked for the psychologist's report – again searching for clues

– but I couldn't lay my hands on it. So I wrote to the psychologist to tell her what had happened and to ask if she could send me the report. This is what she wrote back to me:

> I remember JP as a reserved, loving and kind boy. He was extremely well-mannered. The one thing in my process notes that really stands out is his love for his family – he saw his family as a unit but was particularly close to you, Kate. At that stage, in November 2007, he still felt sad when speaking about his grandpa who passed away when he was eight years old. When I asked him what he did when he felt sad, he said: 'I only feel sad... I never cry.' I remember discussing this with you during the feedback session... he wanted to appear stronger than he felt. JP's favourite animal at that stage was an eagle. The reason was simple: 'It can fly, see things from a distance and is completely free.'

In the report itself, one comment indicated that 'he seems to be dependent on external motivation and praise'. In addition:

> There are 8 points' difference between John Peter's verbal and non-verbal functioning which is not statistically significant. It however indicates a higher level of development of his visual-motor perception and coordination skills as opposed to his auditory processing abilities and concept formation. A discrepancy between John Peter's non-verbal and verbal functioning in favour of the non-verbal scale might indicate that he could struggle with learning subjects. It might also be an indication of learning problems. The presence of intra- and inter-test scatter is noted on two of the three scales possibly indicating erratic attention, anxiety and frustration.

But the psychologist ends with:

> John Peter seems to be a bright boy with a beautiful personality. He definitely has intellectual potential for coping in a mainstream

classroom environment. The possibility of mainstream education can therefore be considered for 2008 (Grade 6).

As I read the report, I note that his auditory-processing abilities are lower than his visual-motor perception and coordination skills, and I am taken back to one of the countless books I have read on suicide – *An Autopsy of a Suicide Mind* by Edwin Schneidman, the most famous suicidologist in the world. This is an in-depth and detailed study of the suicide of a man, drawing on the memories of his parents, his siblings, his ex-wife, his girlfriend and his psychiatrist and psychologist. And I recall that, like JP, this man only started talking when he was three, and that he was also tested and found to have below-average auditory-processing abilities. He had a passive father and forceful mother, and his parents also divorced. He first tried to kill himself when he was fourteen years old. He finally succeeded when he was in his thirties.

Were the planets simply aligned in a particular way on the night my son was born? For who he was – a sensitive, kind and caring child – were the pressures of the lives led by his parents too overwhelming for him? And I smile even as I write those words. How arrogant we are as parents to believe that we have such power, that our actions can cause a child to no longer want to live – as if that child isn't his own person. I am left with a sense that Schneidman, being a medical man who dedicated his life to studying the phenomenon of suicide – and, may I add, never experienced a suicide of anyone close to him – believes that with the right psychiatric and psychological interventions suicide can be prevented. As if life is the only option regardless of how excruciatingly difficult, overwhelming, bleak and dark, scary and frightening, and relentlessly painful it is. For human beings on this planet called Earth, life is so mysterious and most of it is inexplicable, and yet we dedicate our lives to trying to make sense of it instead of embracing the mystery and the unknowable.

The Anam Cara school closed its doors at the end of John Peter's year there. From there he went, at his request, to a small boarding school in the bushveld for Grade 6 and most of Grade 7.

For the remainder of Grade 7, he attended a home-tutoring centre within walking distance of our house. He then went to the local high school for Grade 8 and the first term of Grade 9. But he was never as happy at school as he had been at Anam Cara. For years afterwards JP used to say, 'That year at Anam Cara was the happiest year of my life. Can't you find another school like that for me?' In fact, just days before he died he mentioned the school and how happy he had been there. Several times just before he died he came up to me at inappropriate moments – as I was on my way to shower or as I was leaving for work – and he'd ask, 'Can I go back to the home-tutoring centre? Can I go back to boarding school?' and I'd say distractedly, 'No, John Peter – you can't go back there, and you know why you can't go back there. Why are you asking? You will stay at your school until the end of Grade 10 at least.' Sometimes I'd ask him, 'What's wrong, John Peter? Why do you want to change schools?' and he would give his stock response: 'Nothing.'

I didn't really say it but I did think it: *JP, how can you ask to go back to boarding school?* I found it so strange. Near the end of the first term of Grade 7 he sent me a 'please call me' text nearly every day. When I'd phone him, he'd ask if he could come home or when he could come home. But that was pretty much all he would say. He offered no explanation. He said nothing was wrong but he wanted to come home. Although some weeks were better than others, it was obvious that he was unhappy. And then, near the end of the third term, I got a phone call from the headmaster, who, in the midst of a long rambling monologue, told me that 'John Peter has been caught stealing'. The story had many complicated twists and turns, but after hearing the word *stealing* I wasn't really concentrating – all I could think was, *What on earth is going on?* It was all a bit surreal to me. From what we could eventually ascertain, JP had stolen a considerable amount of money from the headmaster's wife, who was giving him extra lessons in her house in the afternoon. According to the headmaster, small amounts of money were going missing, and then finally I think they must have trapped him and he'd taken R1 000 from her purse.

The headmaster, already suspecting JP, confronted him and asked if he'd taken the money. As Boy does, answering without an iota of self-preservation or guile, he said, 'Yes', and upon the headmaster requesting him to do so, he went and fetched the money. David drove up to the school and brought Boy home – which is exactly where he wanted to be. I am not sure whether he orchestrated events so that he would be sent home or whether stealing the money was a desperate attempt to say 'I don't want to be here anymore'. Or had I not given him enough money and he just wanted money to go and buy stuff at the shop with the other kids? Earlier in the year, one of his friends was caught on camera stealing from the local garage cafe, and JP had been with the group of kids but he hadn't been caught. We were told about this and had spoken to him about stealing and he had sounded quite sure of himself when he replied that he would never steal and he wasn't stupid. So why does a thirteen-year-old steal from a woman who is helping him with his homework?

At the end of the first term at boarding school, when his unhappiness had started, I wanted to bring him home, but David said he must stay and get through the year. I also said to Boy time and time again, 'You can come home if you can tell me why. We can't just take you out of the school for no reason. There must be a reason. Please tell me what is going on. Give me a reason, please, Boy. If you tell me what's wrong, you can come home. Is somebody hurting you? Are you being bullied? What is happening? I promise I won't tell anyone if something is going on. I will just come and fetch you.' Of course in hindsight I realise he would never have told me. He couldn't – he was incapable of that sort of expression. He was non-verbal, inarticulate and confused about his interior emotional life. But something did happen to him there, of that I am certain.

His roommate Lebusa phoned me one night and said: 'I don't know what's happening, but JP is on his bed and hitting the pillow and acting really strangely and he won't talk and he's having like a fit. It's like he's crying but no sound is coming out.' Then I spoke to Boy and he acted as though he was fine. I was worried. I phoned the housemaster, and he went and spoke to Boy and he seemed to calm down. I spoke to Boy again, but he just said he was fine but wanted to come home. He then asked me straight out, 'When can I come home?' He was also cross with me for phoning and involving the housemaster. Was he embarrassed? Was the housemaster the source of his anger and unhappiness?

I do have some regrets in relation to JP, and my lack of action that night is one of them. I wish with all my heart that I had got into my car right away and gone to fetch him. Something was definitely wrong. David went to see a psychic after Boy died, and she told him JP was abused at the school. Perhaps that is why he didn't want to talk about things. Even now as I write – and I ask his permission before I write – I know he doesn't want me to say too much about this time. It's too painful, too shameful, even from that faraway place where he is now. In any case I don't know and I will never know what happened to my boy there.

And then I find the writing. Boy had phoned to say he had left one of his school books at home on a weekend visit and would I go look for it. I go into the family room, where there are lots of books, and I search for the book he asked for. I find an exam pad and open it and see pages of writing with the words *fuck* and *kill* and *death* and *hate* and *sword* and *mask*. It is angry writing and first I think it is Annie's and then I read more carefully and I realise it is John Peter's. I am shocked and very disturbed. The anger, the violence, the aggression almost overwhelm me. It is difficult to read the words and to know that my son has written them. The heavy pen nib marks that stab the pages all the way through the exam pad are so, so angry. I wish I could find these pages now. I am certain that I kept them and hid them carefully where they wouldn't be easily found, as I didn't want to embarrass him. Did I perhaps throw them away? I speak about the writing to my therapist at the time, and a close friend consults her therapist, and both concur that his angry, aggressive words are not cause for concern and that they sound like normal teenage anger. I am told that he was 'getting it out' and 'expressing himself' and that this was good. If he was bottling it up inside, then it would be worrying.

I go through his primary school reports as part of the search for clues – any clues – to his tragic end. Was there a comment I missed? Will I find the key?

His school assessment in Grade 0 reported excellent memory and reasoning skills but below-average spatial and coordination skills. 'John Peter's drawing of a person was adequately integrated but poor structure for his age and showed possible emotional signs.' I'm sure it showed emotional signs, as this test was done when David and I separated… for the second time.

His Grade R report: 'Shy and reserved but very cooperative. Loves to be part of a group – is an obliging friend.'

His boarding school report: 'A pleasure and likeable pupil. He is popular with his peers; if only we could persuade him to develop more "drive"!!' And: 'JP needs to be constantly motivated; however, he is capable of good work.'

And his first primary school report: 'John Peter is working well, but he needs to increase his pace so that work is completed on time. He gets things done in a quiet manner.'

No surprises here – these words describe the boy I know.

21

About six months before Boy died, he took to reading about medicinal herbs and asking me about them. He borrowed all my books on herbs. I am not sure if he was being purposefully disingenuous when he asked me to take him to the nursery to buy herbs. Any interest that John Peter showed in anything I responded to, because so little seemed to interest him and he made so few requests. So we went to the nursery and bought some herbs. He chose rather unusual ones – not parsley and basil, but lemon balm, sage and a variegated mint – and he planted them as soon as we got home. He watered them diligently.

Little did I know that he had also planted dagga seeds at the back of the house, behind Fikile's room, next to the compost heap and behind the washing line – not a secret place, but out of my immediate line of vision. He watered these seeds at the same time that he watered his newly planted herbs. As happens when seeds are planted and cared for, they grew large and lush. Soon a verdant patch of dagga plants appeared. It was inevitable that eventually his carefully nurtured dagga plants would be spotted. But when they were first discovered, I could not remove them right away. Instead I felt tremendous relief that he had taken the initiative to create and care for a garden, even if it was one of dagga plants. Eventually we pulled out the plants in an attempt to show John

Peter that we could not condone illegal activities. But as a friend put it, 'It must have been like destroying your son's hand-built model aeroplanes'.

Soon after JP died, the girls discovered that he had rescued one plant and carefully hidden it on Fikile's roof, continuing to nurture it. The girls cared for that plant until it died, about a year after Boy's death.

My mother wrote to me:

> I think again about the smoking paraphernalia in John Peter's corner of the garden at the back. There were about five various concoctions of plastic containers, smoky pipes within bits, sort of joined together. I was shocked and put it all in the bin. Sitting here now and remembering it makes me think that Boy had drifted away… far away from reality. And now I feel tearful again and very sad. Did he know what was lying ahead? What hardship? That corner was, I suppose, his sacred place. What dreams did he dream there, what insights did he reach?

As far as we can ascertain, JP started smoking dagga in Grade 8, and in the third term I received a phone call from his school: 'Your son has been caught with dagga and is dealing.' I was at work at the time and I fell apart – it was such a shock. I phoned David and asked him to please deal with the school and his son. I was too devastated to do anything. And I hated being cross with my Boy. I knew that by the time I got home I would be able to be loving and generous in my questioning and support of him. But we all believe that what transpired that morning at John Peter's school contributed to his ongoing sense of displacement, alienation, isolation and disconnectedness.

When David arrived at the school, he found his fourteen-year-old son sitting on a chair in the reception area, a public space through which staff and pupils pass regularly, with an armed policeman on either side of him. David remembers JP's demeanour as he sat there – he said it was as though Boy had shut out everything that was happening, as though he didn't care.

But I think he had retreated behind his stone wall for protection from the humiliating onslaught. When eventually David and Boy went into the deputy head's office with the head of Grade 8 and the policemen, the deputy head triumphantly produced his evidence, which David estimated as half a thimbleful of dagga. The policemen laughed at the ridiculous amount and said there was no possibility of a prosecution (this without even weighing it, which is how prosecution is determined), and then they left.

It seems to David and me and his older sisters that the deputy head was deliberately intimidating, humiliating and scaring our son before it had even been established whether a crime had been committed. That the school involved armed policemen when John Peter was underage and caused no threat to anyone was particularly insensitive.

The circumstances surrounding this incident, as told to us by the deputy head, were that a girl at school ordered dagga from Boy on Mxit. This girl showed the message to the head of Grade 8 on the Tuesday of that week. The teacher waited the whole of Wednesday and set a trap on Thursday involving the police. Why, when she knew on Tuesday what was going on, did she not inform us immediately so that we could intervene and work with the school to resolve the situation? Why were the police called? Why were we not informed of the situation on the Wednesday? The incident had entrapment stamped all over it.

David says that during the first encounter with the police and later at Boy's hearing, the deputy head and Grade 8 head were nothing short of vindictive, bullying and unprofessional. Their behaviour was very damaging. David asked questions at the hearing and was not given answers; he was completely ignored. The outcome of the hearing was that Boy was put on probation.

The way that John Peter's school handled this and further incidents is shocking. All I wanted – and still want – is for the members of staff who bullied my son to be held accountable. It's what we all want as a family. I also want staff members not to be able to act in a unilateral way. If police are to be called onto school property, surely the headmistress should be informed first. And in a case like this involving two Grade 8 pupils, perhaps a better strategy would have been a meeting with the parents to discuss an approach that would not have such damaging ramifications. If we had had the support of the school, perhaps Boy would still be alive.

David took Boy for a drug test after the dagga bust and it came up positive. We spoke to him and we took away his privileges – visiting with friends, cellphone, computer access and pocket money. We monitored him carefully.

Sometime after the dagga incident, Boy came home from school one day and told us that a teacher – the same teacher that had 'busted' him with dagga and accused him of being a dealer – had undertaken a written survey with the children in his class. The children were asked to write down a list of names of fellow pupils they don't want to have in their class next year. The teacher (who was a substitute teacher for the class and also happened to be grade head) took in the written scores and after a quick tally proceeded to read the results to the class. Boy and another child received the worst results. John Peter told us this story in his usual monotone voice – as if he were describing an incident that happened to another child, not himself. But of course this must have been a deeply humiliating and embarrassing experience that hurt him deeply. JP was a child who already had low self-esteem and who thought the whole world hated him and was against him.

As I reflect on this incident, I am keenly aware what it must have taken Boy just to tell us about it. I wonder if he even knew that what had happened is not okay. Perhaps he took it as just another of many unpleasant experiences that did not do much more than confirm what he already knew – life is sore. At the time I was furious and wanted to march down to the school immediately and attack the teacher. Or at the very least make a phone call and express my views very clearly. I asked John Peter if he wanted me to intervene, and he said no. I'm sure he thought a mad mother would just make school life more difficult than it already was. Or perhaps he feared further victimisation. I didn't want to make it worse for him. I knew he wanted to stay under the radar – although the dagga incident put paid to that. Annie and Laine, however, were not so easily put off. At school the next day they demanded a meeting with the teacher. They wanted to ask him what he hoped to achieve from the survey. He didn't honour the appointment. They tried to reschedule a few times and then gave up. I am still angry with myself that I didn't go in to request an explanation and demand that the teacher be disciplined for putting children through such a humiliating exercise. I am sure it all had to do with the dagga incident.

Three months after JP hanged himself, the girl who set him up for the bust also hanged herself. Two children are dead. Surely a different outcome may have been possible had the school dealt with the situation in a firm yet humane and compassionate way. Instead, due to the shotgun approach by said teachers, my son got new-found respect and street credibility among his peer group and the girl became a pariah.

Laine and Annie were both in matric at Boy's school the year he died. Annie left the school soon after because it was too distressing for her to be in the vicinity of these two teachers. Before she left, she wrote a letter to the two teachers she believes made her brother's life at school untenable. She was very angry – and still is – about the whole affair.

> 19 May 2011
>
> To: ———
>
> I am writing this letter as I'm sure you STILL do not know what you did to my brother John Peter so I am therefore going to write it down so maybe you realise what you did.
>
> My brother came to ——— High in 2010 and took pride in going to school and wearing his uniform. He was a quiet boy who didn't need to say much. He had a deeper understanding of people than what met the eye. He was conflict free and an observer. He had a kind, generous nature and had a great willingness to help out, as well as a strong reassuring presence. He never went out of his way to make someone else's life terrible as he was obviously in pain and understood how 'the slings and arrows of outrageous

fortune' can hurt. But due to him being quiet people would pick on him… people like YOU.

We spent our whole lives trying to build up his character and help him to fit in. He was known amongst family and friends as 'our boy'.

What did you do? You had a Grade 8 class for substitution… you then went out of your way to make the class vote for who they didn't want in the class and you then proceeded to read the votes out aloud… my brother getting 15 and another child getting 17! In my opinion what you did was violent and abusive.

So while we were trying to build him up and he was at a new school in Grade 8 trying to fit in and find new peers, you went and did that unheard-of vote. I can't believe any grown man who has the privilege to teach children would do such a thing. Laine and I tried to meet with you but you never arrived. We wanted to protect our brother from you – there is something very wrong when a child has to be protected from a teacher. You then continued picking on my brother throughout his time at school.

There are no bullies amongst the school pupils but there are bullies amongst the staff.

And like I said, you made the pain of living for my brother harder and the decision to kill himself easier. You went out of your way to do that vote not knowing how stable or not a child is… not just my brother… what about the other child? My brother already thought he was hated by everyone and he didn't know why, and for you to have done what you did just confirmed for him that he was hated.

I can't believe that you are a father with a son of your own and that you did what you did to someone else's son. It's unnatural for a father to bury his son, but I can confidently say that you contributed to my father having to bury his only son, and a mother losing a child, and a six-year-old sister not really knowing why something like this happened and losing her best friend, as well as me having to carry on without a brother or a best friend, and for an older sister to have to wake up every morning to go to school and see you knowing what you did. You have increased the pain that we are going through as a family and you will never know how much pain it is.

I'm not saying my brother hanged himself because of just you – I would not flatter you so – but you added to the pain and made it worse for him to be alive on this earth. I would also like to let you know that I found my brother hanging and every time I close my eyes that's the only image I have... all I can see is my brother hanging.

I hope you realise what you have done now and that hopefully this is the biggest wake-up call of your life and from it you learn compassion and love for children... If you don't, then you should stop teaching as in my opinion you damage children.

Annie Butler

Laine returned to the school, but after the second suicide and still no action or even a response from the headmistress in terms of raising awareness around teenage depression and suicide, she was also too traumatised to continue attending class. As she put it, '——— High is not a family, it's a lie, families don't treat each other like this... [That school] is no longer a safe place for me.' She is, however, prepared to assist in any way possible to transform this tragedy into positive action. Laine somehow got through matric with excellent results – I really don't know how – without attending classes for most of the second, third and fourth terms.

The school newsletter announcing John Peter's death made no mention that he was a pupil at ——— High and that his death was by suicide. At the time this was like a slap in the face and a sign of great disrespect for my son. I am sure it was also an attempt to keep the manner of his death as quiet as possible. When a pupil at another school died from inhaling deodorant, the school wrote a letter to all the parents and other schools detailing the incident in an attempt to raise awareness so similar incidents could be avoided.

Although I have asked many times what steps the school is taking to ensure that learners and staff receive adequate counselling, I still haven't gotten an answer. There is so much work that needs to be done with the learners around depression and the very real risk of suicide. I am still waiting for a formal response from the school about action taken to hold the two teachers accountable and a change to school policy so that in future no other Grade 8s are humiliated and intimidated like Boy was. I still want to know what the school is doing to ensure staff are sensitised and informed about teenage depression and suicide. I want to know what steps the school has taken to protect children against abusive, damaging and life-threatening actions by teachers. I want the school to know that three suicides in less than five years is *not okay*. But I don't get a response.

And yet, although there was the dagga bust and his name was right there at the top of the teacher's survey in his Grade 8 year, in other ways it seemed to me to be a happy, positive year. I found a couple of sentences I wrote in my journal: *14 January 2010: JP seems very pleased with himself. I think he really likes it at his new high school. Maybe he will finally come into himself and find a place where he belongs.* I wrote this at the same time JP wrote his note that Annie found about wanting to run away. Again I am struck by how much JP kept hidden and even as I thought I knew him I hardly knew him at all. Laine, Annie and JP used to walk to school together looking like triplets in their school blazers. They appeared to be close and good friends. David and I both felt comforted that those valkyries – JP's big sisters – were there to protect him if anyone tried to mess with him. We all felt protective towards him. Even in primary school (in fact, especially in primary school) he needed looking out for. He was shy and awkward and didn't quite fit in. He mostly made friends with the black kids in the class, and he always had one or two really close black friends. They were his mates, these unspoiled and undemanding children of domestic workers. I think he felt comfortable with them. They didn't judge him and he could just be himself without the showing off and the one-upmanship that is common among the wealthier, more 'entitled' middle-class kids.

Boy's best friend was Thando. Thando was his other half, the person always by John Peter's side. Thando is the son of Grace, the domestic worker from next door. We moved into our Greenside house when John Peter was four years old and from then on Thando was his shadow – or was Boy Thando's shadow? At any rate, they were inseparable. When Boy got older, he spent many weekends at Grace's in her back room – Boy, Thando, Thando's sister Bongi and Grace sharing the small, cramped room of a domestic worker right next to the large double-storey house of the employer. And if Boy wasn't next door, then Thando was at our house. That friendship was important to him, and we valued it too.

22

Memory plays strange tricks on us. But because the 'bust' and its aftermath were so painful, perhaps it is not surprising that I had forgotten the 'special', 'confidential' report that JP was asked to take home to us at the end of term three. When I came across it after Boy died, I read it in shock:

> Struggles to socialise... a loner... received a distinction in term 1, withdrawn... apathetic... passive aggressive... distant / slow to respond... total lack of animation... has deteriorated seriously since the beginning of the year... leans back in class with a bored stare... does the barest minimum under sufferance... I have suspected depression... finds it impossible to articulate anything meaningful... I tried to contact his mother – but she hasn't responded to my message...

As I read what the teachers have written, I cry from a place of such devastation I wonder if I will ever be able to stop. I blame myself for not paying enough attention to this report. What sort of mother doesn't take action when presented with something like this? I feel sick to my stomach, my bones ache, my muscles are sore, my teeth are clenched as I whip and lash myself into a frenzy of despair and self-recrimination. The voice in my head says over and over: *Did I neglect him? Why didn't I do something? It's all there… The teachers could see it; why didn't I?*

I stumble around the kitchen, dazed and confused. Why didn't I do something? That question becomes a mantra slowly driving me insane. And then I remember: Of course it was the dagga smoking and those teachers knew and yes, he probably was bored and listless and so on. I was angry with the school when the report arrived and my response was a defensive one. *It's because of the dagga bust*, I say to myself. They wouldn't have noticed anything about him if he hadn't suddenly been thrown into the spotlight and instantly become the most well-known Grade 8 pupil.

I knew he was smoking dagga at the time, and so the report read like that of a fourteen-year-old who has been smoking dagga. It wasn't unfamiliar – this is how I experienced Boy: disconnected. So the report wasn't really a shock to us then, although it is a shock now. We observed a change in him after the dagga bust – as though he had lost interest completely and had withdrawn to some haven in his mind where he felt safe and out of reach. In term four we did a follow-up drug test. When the results came back negative, I breathed a sigh of relief and I thought we were back on track, that the crisis had been averted. We kept a closer eye on him. I found an extra maths teacher and Boy started intensive extra maths lessons.

David and I went to the parents meeting in term four for a report-back on the previous term and it was unhelpful. It was as though the teachers who had contributed to the confidential report had nothing to say other than JP must try harder and make more effort. The lack of connection and genuine relating at those parent/teacher evenings was palpable. It was as though we weren't flesh-and-blood human beings standing in front of them but rather some sort of one-dimensional cut-out cardboard figures. The stock responses peeled off their tongues and I wanted to shout: *Do you know who my son is? Have you ever bothered to find out? Or have you labelled him and put him in a box to react to, much like you are doing to me now?*

Near the end of 2012 I showed the 'confidential report' to a friend of mine who is a high school teacher at a private school and she was horrified. She said that at her school a confidential report is exactly that – confidential – and it is an internal document not handed over to parents. She was further outraged by the fact that the report was given to John Peter to take home. She told us that at her school an urgent meeting would have been set up and the comments in the report discussed with the parents. A path of action would have been decided upon between the parents and the teachers, and follow-up meetings would have taken place. She said the way the school had dealt with JP's situation was careless in the extreme.

It's hardly surprising that JP didn't like school. It must have confirmed all his fears and anxieties about the world as an unsafe place. And yet he got a completely adequate end-of-year Grade 8 report and he even passed maths. We took him to a drug counsellor, who said JP was like any other teenage boy and that he was experimenting and that it is almost impossible to tell who will become an addict and who will just smoke a bit and carry on with life. The counsellor did tell JP that he should ask us to make an appointment if he ever felt depressed or wanted to talk. But Boy never asked to see the counsellor again, despite my reminders that the counsellor was there and I could make an appointment at any time. All he ever asked for was Ritalin in the second half of Grade 8 – his sister was taking it. What would have happened if I had taken him to a psychiatrist and said that my son wanted Ritalin? Would he have been tested? Would depression have been diagnosed? I did go through the checklist for Ritalin for Boy, but I didn't get many ticks and so came to my own conclusion that Ritalin wasn't the solution for him. Perhaps it's just that I simply didn't know what to do. In some inexplicable way JP left me feeling impotent.

Still, his report at the end of the first term of Grade 9 – just before he hanged himself – was a reasonable one for John Peter. He scored in the seventies for two subjects, which for Boy was good. He also failed two subjects. He failed maths, but that had also happened in Grade 8 and with extra lessons he got through, so we started his extra lessons again. The other subject he failed was his favourite subject, social sciences. He said he failed because he hated the teacher and so I was not worried, although I let him know I was not happy about the failed subjects. Later I heard him on the phone to his gran telling her his results. It was clear he was very proud of his report. If only he had failed in a spectacular way or his report had indicated that he was seriously not okay, but it didn't – it could have been the average school report of many fourteen-year-olds.

23

A week or two before JP dies, a strange thing happens. David and I are sitting on our front stoep. It is mid to late afternoon. Boy comes out of the house and David asks him to feed the dogs. There is nothing unusual in this request, as Boy usually feeds the dogs over weekends. (He may have to be reminded, but he does it.) This time he says yes and walks past us with determination and intent. We are left sitting on the front stoep shouting ineffectually after him, 'Boy, where are you going? You must feed the dogs', but he just keeps walking and doesn't turn around or look at us. He opens the driveway gate and walks out. We look at each other a bit nonplussed. 'What's going on with him? Did he just do what we saw him do? How odd,' we say to each other. We wonder if we should follow him, but we don't. When dusk creeps up on us, Boy still hasn't returned. David goes out in the car to buy cigarettes. He says he will drive around the neighbourhood and look out for him. Annie goes along for the ride. I stay sitting on the stoep.

About ten minutes later Boy walks through the driveway gate. I look at him and his eyes are glassy and I say, 'You're stoned! Have you been smoking dagga, Boy?' I get up and say, 'Let me look at your eyes – you're stoned. Where have you been? Why are you stoned?' Then David and Annie get back. David says he was driving down the road and he saw Boy and Bongi sitting at the bus stop. When John Peter saw the car he jumped up and tried to hide behind the bus-stop shelter. But David says it was a stupid thing to do because he had already spotted him and it was too late to hide and surely Boy knew that – so why did he try to hide?

When David pulled up at the bus stop, both he and Annie asked him what he was up to. 'Boy, what are you doing? We saw you. Why are you trying to hide? What on earth are you doing? Why are you at the bus stop with Bongi? Go home now.' And so Boy walked home. We are all on the stoep trying to talk to John Peter and Annie takes out her cellphone and starts filming the ensuing interactions. She is laughing, finding it all very funny. But what is so funny? That fact that she is filming us and we don't really notice or the fact that JP has been busted? Or the fact that she has ineffectual parents who don't know what to do with their stoned son? Stoned John Peter and his irate parents. We lay on the questions and comments: 'Why are you stoned? Why are you smoking dagga? Don't you know that you have the sort of personality that shouldn't smoke? It is dangerous to smoke dagga when you are so young because it can cause schizophrenia when you are a young adult.'

Annie made a series of four cellphone-camera video clips of the conversation with JP around this incident. I have transcribed what I can hear in the clips in case it provides a clue to those last few weeks. In case I spot something I missed. In case I have an a-ha moment. In case there is something, anything, there. If I listen enough, maybe I will get some clarity. As I transcribe the interviews I can hear his voice again… over and over:

David: It's so stupid at your age.
Boy: Well done.
Annie: You fucking stoned, Boy.
Boy: No, I'm not.
Me: I'm talking to you, Boy.
Boy: What?
Annie: Now that Dad has caught you, Boy, how do you feel?
Boy: I don't give a fuck.

Annie: But you do.

Boy: I don't.

Annie: Are you feeding the dogs now – four hours later?

David: Where you scoring the dope from?

Boy: What?

David: Where you scoring the dope from?

Boy: I'm not scoring dope.

David: He's standing there at the bus stop, I come along, he hides behind the bus stop and he says, 'Oh [something]' ... people hide for a reason... because they don't want to be seen.

Me: Your daddy is taking you to be tested next week and you're not coming to AfrikaBurn with us, you're staying here with your father.

Boy: That's the way life is.

Me: And you're not getting pocket money this month and I'm taking your cellphone away from you again.

Boy: Do it.

Me: And no computer.

Boy: Do it.

Me: Give me your cellphone now [mumble].

Boy: It's in my room.

David: I just don't know why you have to go and do it... it's just stupid... You're not doing your homework... We get messages every day... that your books have been forgotten, that your homework is not done...

Me: I wanted to take you to Sci-Bono [Discovery Centre in Newtown] yesterday. You used to love going there... I don't want Thando here, I don't want Noah here... I don't want Daniel here... All right? And no computer. Until you can pull yourself together... you are fourteen years old.

Boy to Annie: Turn that shit off, man.

Me: All these people, Granny and Hamish and everybody, think so highly of you...

Boy: What's wrong? ... But what... I'm not an idiot.

Me: John Peter, smoking dagga when you are fourteen is a moronic thing to do.

Boy: What's wrong with me?
Me: I've told you, when you are fourteen and you smoke dagga, it changes the chemical composition of your brain.
Annie: Your brain is still growing, Boy.
Me: Can you not hear that?

It's very difficult watching and listening to these short snippets. I cannot help thinking that this is one of our threshold moments with Boy and we handled it so inadequately. I want him to respond as I take all his 'privileges' away. I want him to know we are taking this seriously and that what he is doing is not acceptable and all he experiences is us coming down on him and treating him like an 'idiot'. I want him to say, 'No, fuck off, you can't do that to me'. I want him to say, 'Please can I go to AfrikaBurn?' to show me that he wants something. That way I can bargain and say, 'Okay, you can have friends, you can come to AfrikaBurn, you can play computer games because I can see you want it – but please say you won't smoke again!'

If I could have this moment back again, could I write a different script? Could there have been a different outcome? Could I have been more loving and understanding and empathetic? If I had asked him, 'What's wrong that you need to smoke dagga?' would he have just looked at me and said, 'Nothing is wrong. Why are you asking me that?' Could I have said, 'I think so highly of you. You are the most precious child to me and I am worried about you and want to help you.' Would he just have stared at me blankly and thought *Idiot*. If we had taken him to be drug-tested the following day, then what? Yes, it would have been positive and then what would we have done? Gone down to the bottom of the garden to his sacred place and found the bongs and the hubbly and thrown them away. I had already thrown one hubbly away into a bin in Newtown – he was smoking flavoured tobacco then – to show him that we don't think hubblies are okay. That hadn't made a difference. Should we have put him into rehab for smoking dagga? I don't know. We just didn't take it that seriously. We didn't think it was okay and we certainly didn't think that Boy, with his personality – quiet, withdrawn, introverted, insecure, low self-esteem, laid-back, etc. – should smoke dagga. We knew it was potentially damaging.

But we know lots of dagga smokers. We know people who started smoking when they were young and who still smoke as adults – and while they may not be high-achieving business executives, they lead adequate lives. I suppose somewhere in our minds we don't really believe that dagga is a lethal drug. Is it? Was smoking dagga the reason JP hanged himself that day? Or was it that we all came down on him so heavily because of the dagga smoking? Or had he been thinking of killing himself long before he even discovered dagga? Was dagga a sort of panacea for him? Did it provide a temporary escape from all the pressure he was under? Self-medicating, it's called.

I wonder what was going through his mind as this conversation was taking place. He was probably thinking that we are all idiots. Or was he sitting there feeling bad and stupid and unlovable and removed and disconnected? He sat there and he said, 'Something big is going to happen.' He said it a few times: 'Something big is going to happen.' He said it as a challenge and a threat. I said, 'What's going to happen, John Peter? What you going to do, Boy?' and he said, 'You will see'. The words are ominous. There's a dark, heavy undercurrent to them and they agitate me. There's something not right with my boy. His challenging tone irritates me. His lack of response irritates me. What must I do with these words? What must I prepare for? Why the challenge? My mind cannot expand to include self-harm. I don't think he's going to try to kill himself. The best I can come up with is that he's going to try to run away. I know he wants to get out of the city and go camping and fishing. He has been asking what routes to take to get out of the city. He has been asking me to phone the campsite we drove past – 'Camp and Fish' the sign said – when we dropped Annie at a music concert near Potchefstroom. I know he is like a taut rope reaching breaking point. But my mind cannot think further than *He's going to try to run away*. So I ask him, 'Are you going to run away?' and he says, 'Wait and see'.

Not long after this incident, he went to his room with the Yellow Pages and then came out onto the stoep and said he was looking for dry-ice suppliers. He started asking where is this place, where is that place. And I asked him, 'What are you looking for?' and he said, 'I want to get dry ice'. 'Dry ice?' I asked. 'What on earth do you need dry ice for?' And he gave his usual response: 'Nothing.'

I recall during 2010 he had asked for dry ice many times. David's response was, 'I will get you dry ice when you tell me what you want it for.' But he would never tell us. We assumed he wanted it to do experiments. John Peter loved doing experiments. I had bought him a basic experiment book when he was younger, and even after he'd outgrown the book he would do them with Ruby, and so we assumed he had in mind some experiment involving dry ice.

David thought perhaps he wanted to make bombs – innocent bombs. When we were in McGregor burying his ashes, we were sitting around talking about Boy and what had happened and trying to make sense of it all, and one of us remembered the dry ice. The alarm bells went off and I Googled 'dry ice' on my BlackBerry. One of the first sites that come up contains the question, 'Do you want to commit painless suicide?'

24

My mother writes:

> Last year John Peter thumped up the stairs with a bag and just missed the white pottery urn on the little wall. Be careful, I said. He stopped and looked around. I pointed to the pot. He put down the bag, reached for the pot and handed it to me, without a word. I understand his wordless request: For heaven's sake, put it somewhere else. And I did, thinking how clever he is and how stupid I am. Today I will put it back on the little wall until next time a grandchild thumps up the stairs... For me there was this dichotomy – the little boy who just could not remember the words of 'Humpty-Dumpty' (no matter how determined his grandmother was) and the sharpness of removing the pot. We talked about 'Humpty-Dumpty' again recently and he tried to remember the words – and still it had not stuck!! We both just laughed...

Laine, Annie, Ruby and John Peter flew down to the Cape at the start of the 2010 December holidays. My brother Hamish, a builder, had offered to have Boy stay with him and his family for a couple of weeks so Boy could help him on a building site. My mother took the girls to Onrus – she was sad that Boy wasn't with them, because she enjoyed his company so much, especially by the sea. David was also irritated that I had jumped at the opportunity for JP to be away from all of us but still with family – getting up early each morning and being gainfully employed, physically working. I always had this sense that Boy should do real physical work and work up a sweat – not from something meaningless like gym but by making something. David had plans to take Boy on a road trip to Namibia, but I was worried that it wouldn't happen – that a job would come up for David and then that would be it, so Hamish's offer seemed the one to take up. It was real, it was soon and it felt right.

Hamish and his wife, Brigitte, both enjoyed having Boy with them for those couple of weeks. He was quiet, undemanding and polite. He even offered to wash dishes, very aware that he was a guest in someone's house. Every day Brigitte made him delicious lunches to take to the building site. Hamish said that the guys on site all liked having him around and that Boy was sharp and on the ball. One day JP went for a walk around Sea Point and got lost – Hamish couldn't believe that he'd missed their road. When I walked with him months after Boy died, he showed me the turning and said, 'This is what he missed – can you believe it?' I said, 'Yes, I can.' I also remember saying to Hamish, 'Boy wasn't wandering about looking for a drug dealer, was he?' And Hamish just guffawed. 'No, he's just a kid,' he said. 'He's just a boy, like any other.'

One day Boy phoned me and asked if he could go to Robben Island. I almost fell off my chair. I was so thrilled that he had asked for something and that he had shown interest in something interesting! I would have moved heaven and earth to get him there. I offered to pay for his aunt and uncle to join him, but they'd already been. So I said to Boy, 'You're going on your own. Hamish will drop you off at the ticket office. There will be a ticket in your name.' And off he went, all on his own.

I often wonder why he wanted to visit Robben Island. I am sure it was not for its political or historic appeal. I think it was the adventure of it – especially the boat ride. He had never been out on a boat at sea before, and the chance to visit an island must have been an exciting prospect. I couldn't get much out of him after the trip, other than it was 'fine'. Hamish told me: 'All that boy needs is a door and to be left in peace. Given a bit of space he'll be okay. Just get him a door and some privacy.'

On our return to Johannesburg after the Christmas holidays, the first thing I arrange is to make his bedroom more private. We brick up the glass door between his and Annie's rooms, and we put in a proper door between his room and Ruby's. So Boy gets his private corner at the back of the house.

We spent Christmas itself with the children at my mother's place in McGregor. JP divided his time between my mom's house and Susan's house, so that he could spend time with Susan's son Cian. He also spent time wandering the streets with his McGregor friends – I'm sure getting up to all sorts of mischief. I remember being anxious about what was going on. I said to Susan, 'Are you sure the boys are okay and not scoring tik from the onderdorp?' I suppose on some level I sensed that he had already drifted so far away and I was trying to find something concrete and understandable to attribute it to. I figured, *It must be drugs*. But Susan just laughed and said that I was being paranoid, and that when the two boys were not at my mom's house they were at her house playing computer games. I once saw JP chatting to a local boy in the street and I asked him what the interaction was about, but as usual he said, 'Nothing – it was about nothing'. Scoring dagga probably – or perhaps it was nothing, but I don't think so.

One evening I walked Susan home and decided to take a walk under the stars in a different direction. This meant I approached my mom's house from a side road and I saw JP and his gang walking towards me. They were all laughing and Boy was swinging a bottle in large arcs, and I saw it was a bottle of wine. As I got closer I said, 'What's that, Boy?' and he said, 'Nothing'. I said, 'It's a bottle of wine. Where did you get it from?' – as if he would tell me. So I said, 'Give it to me,' and he complied. I took it to my mom and said, 'Is this yours?' and she said yes – it was a special bottle of wine so she recognised it immediately. I was furious. I called Boy inside and demanded that he apologise to his gran. Which of course he did, but with no real remorse. 'Sorry, Gran, I won't do it again,' he said flatly. My mom said, 'Just ask next time.' I suppose I recount this story because I was already starting to watch him carefully, trying to work out what on earth was going on with him – but not consciously – it was an undercurrent of concern. And I wasn't bothered much by the act of stealing a bottle of his gran's wine – I saw it as healthy naughtiness, although I'm sure some wouldn't approve. It was his response to being caught that concerned me. He seemed only to go through the motions in a completely disconnected way.

We went to Murraysburg on our way back to Johannesburg – David, Ruby-Rose, JP and myself. It was a long car trip and a very hot day so we stopped at Meiringspoort for a swim. We walked up to the waterfall, and Ruby and I couldn't wait to dive into the cool dark water. David didn't want to swim – nothing unusual about that. But then neither did JP – my water baby, who normally loved to swim. To me that was so strange. There were other teenage boys climbing up the rocks and jumping in from perilous heights and having so much healthy boy fun. I looked at them and I looked at Boy and I couldn't understand why he wasn't stripping down to his shorts and joining them. Or at least diving into the pool to swim with Ruby and me. The water was so delicious and cool and exciting. He just stood at the edge completely disinterested. 'Come, Boy,' I said. 'Come join us.' But he wouldn't budge.

He and Ruby were also at each other the entire car trip, squabbling incessantly. He was completely uncooperative and irritable and he didn't want to engage with her.

We then drove on to Murraysburg, where we spent time with our friends Paul and Jenet, who both adore John Peter – Jenet calls him *Boytjie*. We were there for two nights, and on both evenings Boy flatly refused to join us when we visited at Paul and Jenet's place. He said he would rather stay in our Murraysburg house. It's a rambling old Victorian with five bedrooms and a living room and a dining room, and a kitchen with fly screens painted a deep green and a wood-burning stove, and a pantry with an enormous yellowwood dresser, and shutters on all the sash windows, and a long passage down the middle of the house, and high ceilings, and a sunroom for winter, and a creaking windmill in the garden turning and whirling in the evening wind, pumping nothing but supplying us with a nostalgic Karoo sound. There are fruit trees everywhere on the property – plum, lemon, apricot, pomegranate, nectarine – and a grape vine. And a succulent garden in the middle I add to each time we visit. And no TV, no music, no nothing – and Boy spent two nights there on his own. So strange, I thought again. I walked down the road to Paul and Jenet's house holding Ruby's little hand in mine and just wondered about him – this son of mine so different from the girls. Maybe it was only that. This same boy, who six months previously had spent a few days in Murraysburg in the middle of winter with David and his sisters. I had stayed in Johannesburg to work and to finish writing up my master's thesis. It snowed and they went into the mountains to build a snowman and have snowball fights. JP phoned me at the end of that day and he said, 'I've just had the best day of my whole life'. I remember the relief I felt – first, that he had phoned me of his own volition to share an experience with me, and second, that he had had such a good time. David told me later that he noticed Boy walk away from the play in the snow – he went off by himself. David wondered about that. JP often seemed to be so neutral in his response to experience and life. Yet he told me that he had had his best year at Anam Cara in Grade 5 and his best day in Murraysburg in the snow.

During our few days in Murraysburg, we allowed Boy to drive David's car. We went out of the town so he could drive on the dirt road, and he was thrilled – visibly so. He couldn't believe that he could drive – he was enthralled by his own ability – and he drove well, no stalling, instinctively knowing what to do, as if he'd been driving in his imagination for years. He also asked us during the few days we spent there if he could come and live in Murraysburg. He asked this very earnestly, as if he really meant it. And we took him and his request seriously. David said to him, 'How will you live? What will you eat? What will you do?' And he was able to answer all these questions, like he'd already worked it out. He had a plan.

We told him he couldn't live on his own in that big house at the age of fourteen, but that he could move there when he was older.

For Boy, Murraysburg was a place of no pressure or expectation to be anyone other than completely himself. Little wonder that he fantasised about living there. One year he put his tent up in the back garden and slept out there with no company except the dogs. It seemed a brave thing to do. He spent time at Paul and Jenet's house with their family, and they'd visit farms, go abseiling, take lots of outings here and there, in that wild, dry, ancient landscape of nothing-but-stillness. He'd always come with me on my evening walks with the dogs. Often he would go off walking by himself, collecting old bones, hunting for scorpions, looking for jewels among the shards of glass in the Murraysburg dump. My mother remembers:

> And years later he crawled into my bed in Murraysburg with the Soduko and we were happily chatting, working it out. I remember David standing at the doorway watching us with a big smile. He was quite a big boy by then and still curled up cosily with his gran.

The year before we'd had such a wonderful holiday there. It was the Christmas before Laine went to Argentina for her year-long Rotary student exchange, and we had a Rotary exchange student from Austria staying with us, and my niece Sarah also joined us. So we had a full house. JP was worried that he didn't have a Christmas present for me yet and so I said, 'Draw me some pictures – I love your drawings'. And he asked, 'What of?' I suggested, 'Sit in the backyard and draw what you see.' And so he did. He drew the braai, the cold-store room, the washing line, the dam which we clean out each year and use as a dipping pool, the windmill and the doring trees. He used bold, confident lines. The picture is solid and clear. He also did another drawing for me, and this one showed, I think, what was going on in his soul. I didn't find the drawing disturbing at the time, just rather odd, but after he died I was sitting by the fire in our Joburg house and I looked up and noticed the drawing and was drawn to it like a bee to nectar – I

A peaceful moment – mother and child, captured by Nicky Newman (McGregor, age about 9 months)

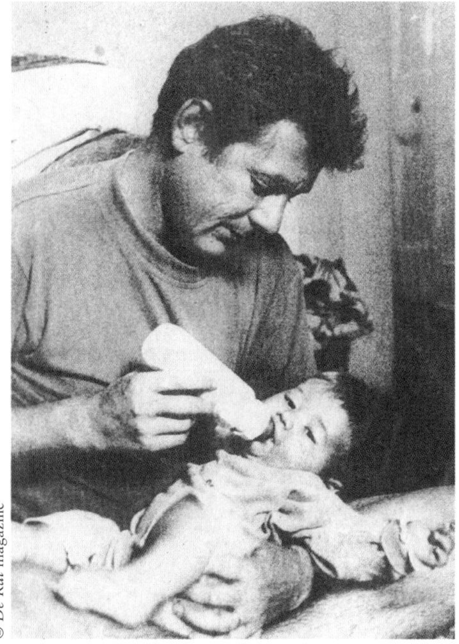

David bottle-feeding JP, as taken by De Kat *magazine (Johannesburg, age about 3 months)*

The six of us posing outside the Murraysburg house (Murraysburg, age 8 years)

JP and Ruby-Rose spent many hours together (Greenside home, age 13 years)

JP and Laine at David's brother's house by the sea (Suiderstrand, Agulhus, age 14 years)

Annie was starting to grow close to her brother and was looking forward to when he was old enough to go out jolling with her – she said he was a "real hotty" (Soweto, age 14 years)

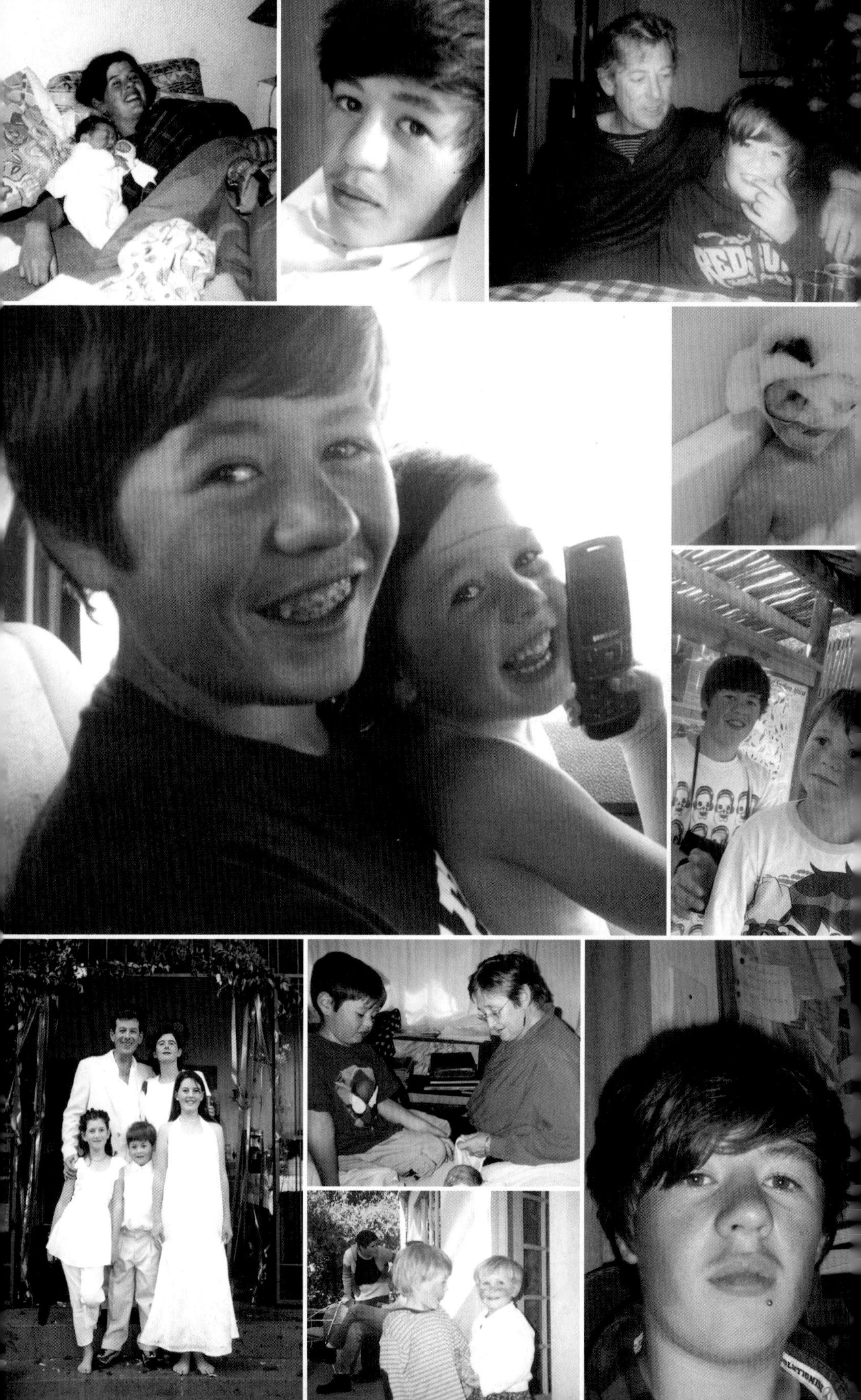

Billabong

Posing for another photograph at the Murraysburg house (Murraysburg, age 12 years)

JP wrote 'JP was here' in black khoki on the wall near the bathroom

A drawing of JP's that we used to create our thank you cards, which we gave to all those who showed kindness to us

Laine's matric final art project is a fabric wall-hanging of her brother's 'journey'

JP's resting place (McGregor)

JP's dying place, in preparation for the marking of the one year anniversary of his death

had found a clue, I was sure of it, if only I could decipher the code. The picture is a bird's-eye view of a boat: the viewer looks down into the body of the boat, where there are two fish fitting perfectly side by side. The perspective of the drawing is unusual, both from above and from the front. The boat in the picture – is it at sea or on land? It is difficult to discern what is land and what is sea, or to identify the shoreline. There is also an image of an aggressive dog – trying to bite the boat perhaps, or barking? An ominous eagle sits in a tree. An arbitrary flower is stuck in the middle of the page like an afterthought. The images are strong and almost biblical – boats and fish. Did Boy perhaps draw a dream he had had?

It was an active and happy holiday. Using stones and mud David and JP built an oven on top of our braai (a few bricks on the earth) and we made pizzas – delicious! David and I went to Matjiesfontein for two glorious nights – a fortieth birthday gift from my friends. Sitting on the grand Victorian stoep watching the trains come and go, with the Langeberg Mountains forming a backdrop. We scratched around in the veld hoping to find some Boer War relic. Instead we found beautiful shards of old glass to add to my collection – seven years previously we had done the same. The children were left alone in the Murraysburg house, although Ruby went to Jenet's house at night. They had a party with some farm kids, jumping in our windmill dam at two in the morning.

On our return we took all the children to Graaff-Reinet to visit the museums. John Peter enjoyed the guns in the Boer War museum. We had a picnic lunch overlooking the Valley of Desolation, and on our way home we made lots of stops for JP and Sarah. Every time they saw something that caught their interest – legavaan, tortoises, roadkill – we would pull over, and we even rode over a snake by accident and squashed its head. To celebrate Christmas, we joined Paul and Jenet and their family at Melton Wold farm outside Loxton/Victoria West. We set up camp on a beautiful patch of green kikuyu grass surrounded by huge 100-year-old shade trees. There was an ancient raised whitewashed swimming pool situated in the middle of nowhere, and the children spent most of their time in or around the pool. I went on a long walk in the veld with JP and we spotted herds of impala and the odd baboon. We experienced the silence, and our imaginations were stirred. We came upon a colonial manor house – it was like a movie set – and found some old graves. Boy examined each one, sharing with me who had died.

JP loved being in nature. It enveloped him and made him feel at peace. In the evenings we watched the cows being milked – large buckets of warm, frothy milk were carried back to the guest house for baking and breakfast the next morning. There were animals everywhere: pigs, sheep, cows, tortoises, impala, eland. We took a long drive through the veld past an old diamond mine and on to an ancient fossil site. It was reconstructed in cement so that we could get an idea of the creatures that used to roam the area. On Christmas Eve we shared our gifts and for the first time I managed to get the 'stuff' under control. I carefully chose second-hand books for everyone and they were appreciated. I gave John Peter some large colourful books on animals. Grace was said before we ate our meals and David did a Bible reading. The meaning of Christmas was clear and the celebration felt focused and contained.

For Christmas Day lunch we went up to the old, unpretentious guest house, which was surrounded by green lawns, roses and old trees. I was invited to travel back to Murraysburg on the back of a friend's motorbike and it was intense and exhilarating – a highlight of the holiday. My long hair hung loose for a change and flowed behind me in the wind. I felt so close to everything. The girls met lots of farm kids and even went to a farm for a party. Just before the new year, we travelled to Nieu-Bethesda for lunch with our friends Jacques and Graeme. Beautiful Nieu-Bethesda overrun with Gauteng number plates – it was all very civilised after the roughness of camping and semi-camping in our old Murraysburg house. On our way back we stopped at the retirement home in Graaff-Reinet to meet Tannie Kay, aged 102 – the previous owner of the Murraysburg house – and her sister Margy, aged 99. That was an extraordinary experience for all of us.

Back in Murraysburg, Annie turned fifteen and I cooked a

special birthday breakfast. In the afternoon we even managed to bake a cake. I preserved figs and made apricot jam from the fruit from our trees. David had found a gardener for the place, so slowly the parched earth was coming back to life. All was not dead on our arrival and it made a huge difference. Olive trees, grapes, pomegranates, lemons, apricots, figs – all were growing. Even a pumpkin popped up out of one of our compost holes. We planted two rosemary bushes, and I started a succulent garden from slips found on nearby koppies and gardens.

We went on a walking adventure to find a farm gate by a big tree, with a key under a stone next to a bossie but the bushes all looked the same and we couldn't find the key. We visited another farm next to a small stream. Some farm labourers' kids walked past with a skinned dassie that they'd trapped strapped to the back of one of them. Stones thrown at mangy dogs sent them yelping home. Reminders of the harshness of the Karoo: a dead horse left in the veld, a tortoise with four back legs. Crystal-clear spring water pumped out of the earth. We visited the old Pophuis farm – it's exquisite and abandoned. The farmer's wife used to be big on honey, Jenet told us. The next day we went back to the farm gate and the key under the rock and this time we were in luck. As we hiked through a forest of acacia and pepper trees, we discovered a cement dam of clear spring water and we took a refreshing swim in it. We walked around this abandoned farm where someone had once lived and farmed. It is now a ghost farm of rusting implements and crumbling walls, all reminders of the past. The Karoo is like one gigantic echo of who we once were. I wondered as I walked if this great silence could consume one and if it overcomes those who scratch out their existence in this harsh, enormous, magnificent silence – terrible beauty, terrifying silence. On New Year's Eve there was Afrikaans music, drumming and dancing (although JP did not take part). It was easy and relaxed. David made a great potjie. JP learnt how to catch scorpions. The four of us – JP, Ruby, David and me – climbed the Murraysburg mountain and reached the sign of white painted stones and beyond.

25

John Peter loved to sleep outside. Many nights the old canvas tent David and I bought when we were newly married would be hauled into the back garden (I thought it was safer than the front garden – out of sight of passers-by) and tied up with bits of anything he could find, and he would sleep in there – usually with Thando. Our house has a flat roof with a staircase to the top, and in summer Thando, Bongi and Boy would make themselves comfy up there for the night. And one winter David and Boy spent the coldest night of the year in the front garden in the cheap old tent. David brought out an electric lead, a bedside lamp and an electric blanket, and he and Boy slept out. On another occasion, Boy and his friends Daniel and Niall slept out in our garage, which doesn't have a door. They made a fire and everything – they were young and it seemed so innocent. But at 3 a.m. our neighbour Di was smoking a cigarette on her stoep. She saw youngsters walking in the street – and when she saw them come through our gate she recognised them. That was the last time Boy was allowed to sleep outside. Looking back, I'm sure sleeping out was good for him. It gave him a sense of freedom, of being in touch with nature – close to the sky, stars and moon and close to the earth – and I'm so sad about stopping his sleepouts. What did they get up to that night as they wandered around Greenside? How much didn't I know about this son of mine? And when we told him he couldn't sleep outside anymore, he didn't fight it – didn't fight me – didn't resist at all. He just shrugged his shoulders as he did and seemed to accept it.

My mother wrote: 'I was also surprised when I found the photograph of him dressed as a girl. Another AH! memory. Poor boy, surrounded by all the girls dressing him up.' But JP loved all the attention. In fact, he loved the attention so much he took an uncharacteristic swagger down the McGregor main road in full drag, prancing and preening and loving every second of it. It was a bit of a shock to see him behave like this – putting on and showing off this female persona. But that was a one-off – he never did it again.

For months before he died Boy asked me for 'soft bedding like Granny has'. I looked for bedding for him every time I was in Woolies or Mr Price but couldn't find anything suitably boyish in pure cotton. His other request was for an eiderdown or duvet that doesn't have a cover, so that you simply wash the whole thing at once. In his mind this was an item of bedding that was soft and comfortable. Strange that a boy who loved to sleep outdoors on the hard ground or on the concrete roof with nothing but a few blankets wanted soft bedding so much. Had his skin become thin and irritable? Eventually I went to the Oriental Plaza and looked for sky-blue percale but only found white. I bought enough to make him a set of bedding and it went into the cupboard for the day when I would get it together. In the end I used it to make Laine a double-bed sheet to add to her duvet cover set for her nineteenth birthday, which was eight days before he took his life.

My mother said to me recently – and not for the first time: 'I am cross with Boy. He did none of us a favour by killing himself. His life wasn't that bad. It really wasn't that bad. Whichever way you look at it, he had amazing experiences. He got to know South Africa so well for someone so young. He went to boarding school in the bushveld surrounded by wildlife, and he had many long holidays in Murraysburg in the heart of the Great Karoo and he had seaside holidays at Arniston and Onrus.' And of course he spent time in McGregor. He got to know these places well and he had friends in those places. He had freedom. He explored, he fished, he built shelters, he climbed trees, he went for walks, he collected fossils, he found old animal bones, he hunted for scorpions, he swam.

My mother writes:

> Thought so much about him on the sand dunes at Arniston. Down he would come, rolling or on a tray and back up again, over and over. Way beyond exhaustion!!! I was always amazed watching that boy on those sand dunes. And I could remember without crying and delight in the memory. Old Josh [JP's cousin] did it a few times and then said he's tired! Told him about JP…

And another letter:

> In my big cupboard I found a tin full of hooks and sinkers – we've had it for years and every time we went to Onrus out it would come and be refreshed. I remember how keen Boy was to go down to the tidal pool to fish. When they were little (too small to go by themselves – always the impatient wait!) he was fisherman and Sarah [his cousin] the assistant. Sarah would go down into the water to collect the bait, crush the shell and thread it on the hook. John Peter would then 'cast' in. A fish would bite and he would reel it in and then Sarah would remove it from the hook. Mostly they threw them back. They would be happily busy for as long as I had the patience. I was always touched and amused by his squeamishness – tender-hearted, I thought. Yet that same boy got a huge burn right across his leg from the biggest bluebottle ever and just jumped around saying 'Ah ah ah ah'. I rushed him to the chemist for muti and they all cringed at the pain he must have been in. For heaven's sake he tore a ligament in his leg here in McGregor and we all wondered if it was serious because he showed so little emotion. Torn ligaments are agony. His leg was black and blue. Do you remember walking back from the beach and John Peter hobbling with wide-apart legs? When we investigated he was chafed blood-raw on his inner thighs, salt water stinging like

> crazy. That day I thought he was very brave. But why didn't he scream blue murder, sit down on the pavement and wait for one of us to fetch the car!!!

John Peter loved his food, especially his granny's food. 'What's for supper, Gran?' he'd ask, and she'd tell him and he'd show great appreciation. 'Oh, that sounds really good,' he'd say. My mother remembers:

> While making supper for Josh I explained to him that it was John Peter's favourite food [when he was little] in Granny's house. I buttered the toast, put the soft fried egg on top, sprinkled cut-up bacon over it, squashed the fried tomato on top and added lots of Worcester sauce. Then cut it all into tiny squares, easy for him to eat. I made it for Boy again in December, teased him a little but didn't cut it up! He was very interested in food. Always asking what's for supper… 'Wow!' he'd say, like it was something special. Wish I had the fish pie recipe that he wanted to show me. Always made sure there was lamb knuckle stew that he loved so much. And so my memories are tied up with food, nurturing, nourishing, sharing, spoiling…

When I turned the family meals vegetarian for a number of years, John Peter would sometimes ask for money and go up to Checkers and buy steak, which he'd marinade in his own magic sauce. Then he would light a fire in the garden outside and braai the meat, sometimes on his own but usually with Thando. David can remember him once asking for a big steak, so he bought Boy one of those Texan specials and Thando, Bongi and Boy braaied it in the garden and jumped over the wall and devoured it in Grace's room next door. Over those first few months of 2011 he cooked a lot for himself. I remember him often marinating chicken fillets and then frying them. He would help Fikile make supper, especially making up marinades and sauces. He was so pleased with himself about how delicious he could make the chicken or beef taste. This was after I'd given up on the vegetarian meals – much to everyone's relief. But I remember how on the morning of Laine's nineteenth birthday – eight days before Boy hanged himself – I got up early to make a special bacon-and-egg breakfast for her. The whole family was sitting at the table. I made lots of whole-wheat toast and a couple of slices of white-bread toast, using up what was left in the packet. I gave Ruby the last piece of white bread and put John Peter's eggs, bacon, mushrooms and tomatoes on a plate with a slice of whole-wheat toast. He asked for white bread and I said it was finished, and then he did something so uncharacteristic. He said that he wasn't going to eat his food and he pushed his plate away. He just didn't seem to care.

He also showed no concern that he didn't have a birthday present for Laine. He was usually so conscientious and anxious about Christmas and birthday presents. He would often come to David or me a day or so before a birthday and say that he had a problem – that he didn't have a gift for the birthday person. We would help him arrange something. His gifts were always well thought out and appropriate for the person receiving it. He was very clear about what he wanted to give.

So I told him that I was giving Laine bedding and would wrap each item separately so that each sibling would have something to give to her. He showed no real interest, just looked up and said, 'Okay'. But I reminded him to make her a card. I had taken his computer privileges away because of his dagga smoking and so he asked if he could go onto the computer to make her card. Of course I agreed and he made her an amazing card drawn on the computer. It was a cartoon strip of Laine learning to drive in the garden. He captured the essence and the humour of those sessions perfectly: David irritated because she kept stalling the car, Annie laughing and videoing the sessions with her cellphone, and Laine frustrated. When I look at that card, I can hardly believe that he was so alert and so in tune and so witty just days before he hanged himself.

When John Peter was in boarding school, he phoned us often and usually the conversations started with him saying, 'There's a problem'. That was JP's mantra. The problem usually involved an Afrikaans essay or some other homework assignment that hadn't been done and we would coach him through it over the phone. And he continued with this 'There's a problem' until he died. Always a problem, never a solution. It was as if he couldn't quite believe that whatever was wrong could be solved. But we always helped him solve it. Until 31 March 2011.

My mother:

> Every now and again Joshua talks about John Peter: 'He shot up crackers with me.' 'He flew the kite with me.' 'We played with the guns and shot at targets, we took turns.' Josh walked with me to my house and in front of Paul's family he announced that he was so unhappy he was going to kill himself, like John Peter. I think of all that cricket that was played on your front lawn, with whoever was willing, and do you remember, Kate, when we took him to the park to kick that ball around? How energetically he ran to fetch it and then kicked it again and again, enjoying you and me watching! And round and round the block on the skateboard – he enjoyed physical exertion. Up the sand dunes, off on the bike. Wish he could have had some big long hikes – those would have come when he was older… I have been trying to put myself in his shoes those last two days. He must have felt so terrible about what he was doing to all of you and that is what he could not face. So it still goes round and round in my mind, but days now pass peacefully and I know the weight of this will become bearable.

David bought a bicycle for the Murraysburg house and I was furious. Why buy a bicycle for a house we hardly spend time in when John Peter needed a new bicycle at home? And one of the first things I did when we got back home in January 2011 was to take Boy to choose a new bicycle. I bought him that bicycle so he could have the pleasure and joy of some independence and get a bit of exercise. We ended up at Game and there were a couple of bicycles to choose from. But he really didn't seem to care which bike he got – in fact, he seemed decidedly unenthusiastic about the entire bike-buying experience.

Once we got the bike home and assembled, however, he just rode it and rode it and rode it. After he died many people mentioned how they always saw him out and about on his bike, but usually going to Checkers. We gave his bike to Thando – Boy had ridden it for only two months.

He was in the car with me one Saturday afternoon shortly before he died – we were driving around Westcliff trying to put Ruby to sleep. We drove round and round in large circles. JP shared with me that he, Thando and Noah had taken their bikes right to the very top of Westcliff and freewheeled down the hill all the way back to our Greenside house. I was secretly delighted that he had done such an energetic and thrilling thing. Once again I reminded Boy about the need to wear a helmet when bike riding, although I knew it was probably futile. Looking back, all that worry about Boy out cycling on the roads of Johannesburg without a helmet seems terribly ironic.

I took JP and Sarah horse riding during the 2010 Christmas holidays. Sarah mounted bareback and rode the horse as though she'd been riding bareback her entire life. JP also mounted bareback, but as soon as the horse moved away he slipped off. When I asked him if he wanted a saddle, he declined with wounded pride and got back on, and although he looked quite uncomfortable he rode that horse without a saddle for an hour and a half. JP had never been on a horse before, but he was determined to ride without a saddle and he did it. It's clear to me that his will was firmly in place.

One Easter I drove to McGregor with just Boy and Ruby. We made the trip in one day listening to Gordon Ramsay narrating his autobiography, *Humble Pie*. I liked that Boy was listening to a story about a person overcoming adversity. Boy was good company on that trip. On the way back I stopped every time he asked me to so that he could examine roadkill. I am so pleased I had the patience to do that.

I recall a funny day shortly before he died. Our home is a bit chaotic – as my mom says, 'There's nowhere comfortable to sit!' In our open-plan area there is a long beautiful wooden table that takes up all the space but we seldom use it. In the TV room there is an ancient in-need-of-repair Art Deco lounge suite, and by the fireplace there are a few chairs. I decided we needed to rearrange the rooms so that we could have a proper 'lounge' area. JP helped me push the long table under the window and move the deco suite into the large room – and suddenly we had our lounge. When we were all done, Boy sat on the couch – actually, he fell into the depths of it because it needed springs and cushions and was tattered and torn – and he said, 'Now we have a house like everyone else!' I remember that remark so vividly. I'm not sure if he said it with satisfaction – as if we had achieved some sort of status – or if he preferred the set-up as it was before. Perhaps it was just an objective observation without much of a subtext. And I smiled to myself – only my boy could think that that tatty furniture could create a house like everyone else's. No other middle-class family would dream of putting such furniture in the centre of their homes. But it simulated a lounge suite and that was enough for him to see the potential.

The furniture was meant to be there temporarily until I repaired it or bought something more suitable. And then JP died and the house was full of people and things were just as they were – the old people thinking they were going to settle into a comfy chair and instead would just about fall through – and I spent weeks apologising for the furniture. But somehow it also seemed fitting that no one could sit comfortably. In fact, the physical discomfort seemed appropriate. This wasn't a place to lounge and relax – after all, people were coming to pay their respects.

Boy practically grew up with Sarah, the two of them looking like twins with their blond hair and suntanned bodies. They were very close when small, always going on adventures and walks around McGregor together, hand in hand; then on their bicycles, doing McGregor-child stuff like catching frogs, collecting stones and feathers, daydreaming, climbing trees, playing in sand, swimming, making mud cakes, going to the shop to buy sweets; and finally as teenagers, just hanging out. Sarah sent me a cellphone video clip of her and Boy up at the McGregor dam. It's disconcerting to watch. He is covering his face with his cap – the ubiquitous cap – and he is saying that he will hurt her, and Sarah is saying, 'But why, JP? Why do you want to throw a stone at me?' and he says, 'You laughed at me,' and she laughs. They're wading through the shallow water, aimlessly repeating the same words – Sarah asking the question and Boy responding, but with no real intention in his voice.

Melinda's boys, James and Daniel, bring me a memory card with all the cellphone video clips they've made. There are close to 100 video clips of a couple of minutes each. There is one that foreshadows what is to come. Somehow these boys made a video of Boy apparently jumping off the roof, after he says, 'I'm going to go and kill myself'. Melinda's boys say, 'No, JP, don't kill yourself.' And he jumps off the roof and without a cut – at least, that's what it looks like – the camera moves to the edge of the roof and there's Boy lying on the ground. Except they had cut it – he'd disappeared over the edge of the roof and then run down the stairs and laid down on the ground. It's a clever little video. It even has a soundtrack.

And then there are the repetitive attempts – over forty of them – to get a handmade potato gun to shoot a potato. Daniel tells me it worked the first time they tried, but they weren't filming then. Over and over they kept trying to shoot this contraption made with a pipe and deodorant and fire. It all looks naughty and dangerous, but not too dangerous, and I cannot believe they try so many times – and all the while they are laughing at each other. Then there is some repetitive footage of petrol being thrown onto a pile of earth in the back garden, and they set it on fire and then try to put it out. It's not clear what they were trying to achieve, but there's much hilarity, and sometimes they can't get the fire out so they shovel earth over it. David says, 'Oh, is that where the petrol for the lawnmower kept disappearing to?' and I think, a-ha, that's how they managed to set fire to the ancient tree stump in JP's corner. I remember I was on the stoep on the phone with Viv, the other Daniel's mom, and I suddenly noticed smoke and then flames. I shouted for Boy and David. I say: 'Boy, the tree is on fire! What have you been doing? Go put it out now!' I put the phone back to my ear and Viv hears me laughing. It's just a boy's prank, and somehow I feel relieved that something, anything, is going on – even if it involves fire.

JP wanted to build a place in the garden that he could move into. Without asking, he started to dig the foundations – he got Thando and Noah to help him. And for weeks every spare moment he was digging, they were digging. I started engaging him on it. Boy said he wanted to lay foundations and build a proper brick room. David was against it – we'd need planning permission, and so forth – but I was just so pleased JP wanted something and was working towards it that, perhaps wrongly, I supported him. I told him that he could build a room but he had to do it himself, and that I wanted to see plans and I would buy the materials. I suggested he make a wooden structure because it would be easier and less permanent. It captured my imagination – a boy building a room for himself. When Hamish came to visit, I asked him to go down to the site with Boy to see what he had planned and if it would work. Hamish was impressed with what JP had planned. He told me that Boy knew exactly what he had to do and that it would work. He said that Boy had worked it all out in his head and the room would be structurally sound.

I asked Boy to draw me the pictures of his plan and measure the pieces of wood and give me a shopping list of what I needed to buy. He did draw it up but it wasn't quite detailed enough for me to know what to shop for, and I didn't really have the money anyway. So I didn't push it, but as I sit writing I imagine Boy with a picture in his head of his own place, his room out in the garden away from the family – his space. Not quite a shelter in the bush on his own, but the next best thing. The dream of a fourteen-year-old boy. And I feel so sad that I didn't take him to Builders Warehouse and buy his wood and that I wasn't more proactive in actually helping him get it done. He could imagine it, he could draw it, he could dig his foundations, but he needed me to take it to the next level. And I couldn't… I didn't.

Instead I suggested a shelter that he could build without spending money or needing planning permission: a tepee. I found a plan for a big tepee and we had the wooden sticks for it. He got the structure right, and then he had to weave branches through to secure it and cover it with plastic. Ruby was also very excited because it would be a space she could use. And so his idea for a brick shelter of his own morphed into a tepee in the back garden that was for Ruby as well, no longer the room of his imagination where he could have privacy and shut the door and create his own sanctuary. He did finish the tepee but without much enthusiasm. On the first anniversary of his death we burnt it on a big bonfire.

David built him a very simple go-kart – the sort of go-kart a young boy from another age would have had – and he and Thando rode it like crazy for months. They would go up and down the driveway or the streets of Greenside and push each other up hills and freewheel down them. A wheel would break off, and they would spend hours fixing it and getting the go-kart back to working order, and off they'd go again. Eventually the wheels couldn't be fixed anymore so they made new wooden wheels – David got out the circular saw and helped them. That go-kart got used until it literally fell apart and couldn't be patched any further. What is left of it is still lying in the back garden. Either David will make something from the scraps or when we light the bonfire again we will burn them.

Boy played rugby, like his grandfathers and father before him. He started playing at Pirates the year he was at Anam Cara. One evening both David and I were late fetching him from practice because of work commitments. Independent of each other we went to the field, but there was no sign of Boy and so we went home. There was Boy. He said he was cold and we didn't come so he walked home. A car stopped and the occupants asked him why he was walking alone in the dark and did he want a lift? So he said yes and got into the car. We were horrified, begging him to never do such a thing again. We told him that he must wait for us because we will always come, and he must never get into a car with strangers. But that wasn't Boy's way. He continued playing rugby throughout primary school and into high school, and David didn't miss a Saturday game and often attended practices if he was available. He was the most supportive rugby dad at JP's school and very proud of his son on the field, especially when Boy actually paid attention and made a move – he often skulked at the back trying to be invisible. He also used to go to the local pub with his dad when there was an important game on, and it was a time of bonding and male camaraderie. One never knew if Boy actually enjoyed rugby or really wanted to play or watch matches; sometimes I think he did it just to please David. But then one never knew with Boy, as his responses were always so neutral.

He wasn't a big reader. In fact, I used to pay him to read books – and then he'd read them, all the way to the end. The rate was about R200 a book, depending on its length. One of his first proper reads was *The Power of One* – I so hoped he would get some strength from that story. Build a bit of resilience. That the story would be a key to unlock his will to carry on and encourage his spirit to overcome challenges. Before he died he read *The Last American Man* by Elizabeth Gilbert (of *Eat, Pray, Love* fame). I didn't have to pay him to read that one; he devoured it. It's about a man who can survive in the wild without any modern implements or comforts. Eustace Conway finally settled down on some land and started a place where anyone can come and learn how to survive in the wild. John Peter found his website and days before he died he came to me and asked, 'Mom can I go to that guy's place in America?' and I knew exactly who he meant. And I said, 'Yes, you can, John Peter – when you've finished school.' Would the outcome have been different if I'd said, 'Yes, you can, John Peter. Let's make a plan to get there as soon as possible'?

He wanted to live on a farm. My mother remembers:

> I don't remember why the silly conversation always came about. Never mind, John Peter, I would say, I'll buy a farm for you and me. We can go far away and live off the land. It was a long-held dream of ours going back to the sixties. We had all read John Seymour's self-sufficiency books and loved the concept. And so when Boy seemed to struggle with homework or I fell back into that escapist mood, the conversation would arise. Then one night the whole family were gathered round the kitchen table enthusiastically making plans and daydreaming of the possibility. John Peter was vociferous that night. Eyes shining brightly. Hands waving. And

> then I did the unforgivable. I played the devil's advocate, pointing out the snags of this so-called ideal life. His face fell and he looked at me and said, 'You always do that, Granny, spoil things.' I tell this with deep sadness and regret. It was like a bucket of cold water on my head and I have tried ever since to leave the young to their dreams. Life will teach its own lessons. Boy and I had this pact from the time he was little until that last visit before he died. And again I cry and feel the huge emptiness that he has left behind in our lives. I loved him deeply, our funny little boy.

Certain adult men responded to John Peter, as if he represented all the pathos and difficulty of being a boy in this world. I remember sitting on the back stoep at the end of an evening braai. Most of the guests had left and a few of us were still not ready for the evening to end. John Peter joined us, and Charles – a heavy-drinking chain-smoking writer – got talking to him. Actually Charles did most of the talking, but every now and then there was an opportunity for Boy to respond. Charles must have been asking JP about school and his subjects and what he felt about them. Boy said that he struggled with maths. Charles said to him, 'You must trust your brain.' And I remember thinking: *Yes, Boy, that's right. How do I help you to trust your brain?*

Shy and introverted as he was, John Peter was prepared to play Fleance to David's Banquo in a production of *Macbeth* at the Joburg Theatre. JP was still young – only ten or eleven – and I thought he was so brave. I was also slightly amazed that he was willing to participate, when at school and among his peers he seemed so shy. And he played his part night after night – even when he got a tummy bug and he was vomiting backstage. He would vomit and then go on stage and say his few words and come back to the dressing room to vomit again. But not once did he say, 'I'm too sick to do this'. It was as if he'd been told this is what he had to do and so he just did it, no argument, no idea that he could actually say, 'I'm sick and can't do this'. Vanessa remembers this time. She was staying with us for a night or two and she also had a tummy bug, and we were all stumbling about late at night as Vanessa was vomiting. She recalls that Boy went and got a bucket for her and helped her – and she says she remembers his kindness that night with such fondness. She also remembers the flower he picked for her on her birthday when he was very little, and also an incident when he was older: 'It was that same vomiting holiday. We were in the car, I was in front, Ruby and Safra [Vanessa's daughter] strapped in the back seat, Boy between them. I turned round, and he was gently tickling Safra's little hand. He saw me looking at him and got shy. Very beautiful little moment...'

26

We gave him fantastic birthday parties when he was younger, usually with a big bonfire and always a treasure hunt. And lots of children, lots of presents, creative cakes. One year my uncle, a sculptor, came at my request and I supplied him with a couple of vanilla sponges, icing and sweets, and he sculpted a magnificent monster for Boy's birthday cake.

My mother writes:

> Now I want to talk about John Peter's birthday. I found photographs that seem to be his first, second, third and fourth. What a serious little boy. No smiles in any of them, but surrounded by family and friends always, special cakes, singing 'Happy Birthday'...
>
> Last year we made a beautiful birthday for him. Cooked big steaks with special sauce by special request and allowed him some champagne. We sang 'Happy Birthday' and kept up the general festive mood! I had a lovely evening, but the next day wondered what he thought. Did he have a good time? I could not read him and I worried about it... I went with him to buy his birthday present at the music shop and he chose too quickly and then took no interest in it afterwards. (Maybe he used earphones!) I wondered if this was what he really wanted. Asked him again about it. I wished

> he would speak up and not just acquiesce with me. And then he surprised me by pointing to the red shirt and saying spontaneously, 'Buy me that shirt'. Why didn't I just do it, why did I have to think about it twice? Fikile tells me he was always looking for it, waiting for it to get out of the wash. My sense of not getting through to him I put down to adolescence.
>
> In one of the photographs, you are leaning over him lovingly and holding his hand guiding him to cut his cake. I think it was his fourth birthday. The cake is a beautiful big cuddly teddy bear. Do you remember it? It was covered in brown coconut (fur) and lying on a bed of green coconut (grass). In this picture all the children are serious – important business of cutting the cake!

He didn't want parties when he got older, although he kept threatening that he was going to have a big party for his fifteenth birthday. My mother wrote: 'Was this the birthday he planned a big party? Would he ever have done it? Or was it just another wish in his imagination?' We were all thrilled that he wanted a party and supported the idea, but he died before that big teenage party could happen.

More from my mother, always so eloquent:

> A very gentle and happy dinner with the family to celebrate Sarah's birthday. I could see her relaxing and enjoying herself. I went to bed feeling happy. And thought about my angst with John Peter's birthday [his fourteenth], also at my house with the family, and how I could not read him at all. Did he enjoy it? Was he content? Did he feel our love? I remember expressing these thoughts to you and to Hamish, who remarked, 'We showed him what family is anyway, it was all good!' Oh Kate, my heart breaks when I think of it. He was locked away somehow – what did he feel? What did he think? Who was he? A year down the line I try to reach out, to remember the essence of him. Does one love so blindly? Or is that love protective of something not fully understood?

Those words of my mother's have stuck with me: 'Or is that love protective of something not fully understood?' Did we love him so much because we knew he needed protection – that he wasn't the same as us?

27

We went to visit the eagles at the Walter Sisulu Botanical Gardens on what would have been Boy's fifteenth birthday, just three months after he died. It was a gentle, peaceful day – just the five of us – David, Laine, Annie, Ruby-Rose and me – lying in the sun remembering our beautiful boy. I think he would have been a really cool fifteen-year-old: he would have started coming into himself – his braces would be gone, he would be shaving, he'd be tall and handsome, he would have a girlfriend, his sisters would be taking him out at night, he'd be quiet but present, making the odd joke, he'd be a cool dude, minding his own business, doing his own thing, taking pleasure in his burgeoning manhood, curious about it, watching it happening almost as though it were happening to someone else.

My mother had written:

> Tomorrow is going to be very hard. I think your ritual to go to the eagles is wonderful – pay homage. Perhaps you can write something (like a prayer) for Ruby's sake, no, for all of you. And then you come home and have the big party for him. Drink champagne and see him soaring like an eagle, strong and free, released from all earthly cares…

On his sixteenth birthday Annie was in Strand and she had to write an exam. David was also there; he had to rehearse in the afternoon and perform at night. Laine was in McGregor. She went to Boy's grave in the early morning with my mother, sister and niece and they planted an aloe. Ruby, Fikile and I were in Johannesburg. Ruby and I took the day off – in honour of our Boy and because we could. Once again the three of us went to look for eagles at the botanical gardens. I invited a few close friends for tea and cake in the afternoon. We lit a bonfire and burnt what was left of his clothes – to release a little more of him and to grapple with acceptance. Acceptance that he's no longer here and that we will never see him on this earth again. A friend left a message on Facebook: 'One day in one moment, suddenly, you will have the overwhelming knowledge that he is there with you. And it will never go away.' I believe her because her brother was killed in a hijacking – she knows. Some days there is a glimmer of this. It is a slight fragile thread of sensing *he's nearby* – and I am comforted because the moment of full knowledge of this will come. I know it will not arrive suddenly but will gently nudge its way up on me and I will hardly notice unless I listen very carefully, but I will awake one morning and there will be peace.

For the one-year anniversary ceremony of his death, Gillian came with brown paper bags and tea-light candles and we cut out shapes into the bags and filled them with sand and a candle and placed them around the outer perimeter of the labyrinth I created in the garden in honour of JP. When it got dark we lit the candles and the labyrinth looked exquisite and magical. Our guests walked it in their own time just because it was there, an invitation to experience intention, clarity and transformation.

To honour him and the anniversary, I transformed the space under the back stoep where he died into a shrine. We swept it out and covered the walls with photographs of him. I brought down the eagle I had sewn from scraps of his duvet and some old clothes and hung it over the security gate he'd used to hang himself. Laine's wall-hanging of her brother's journey, which she made for her matric art class, was also put up, along with Annie's sketches of Boy. I put out a small table and Ruby covered it with a cloth and placed on it a candle and the ceramic angel she made in pottery class. Mom gathered a big bunch of colourful foliage from the garden, and flowers that we were given were also placed there. I asked everyone who came to bring candles so we could bring light into the space. And so, for the special anniversary day to honour and celebrate him, we created a beautiful space.

Early that morning I went to a quiet spot away from the house to write about my son. I hadn't spoken at the funeral and I needed to say words in his honour – for all of us – on this first anniversary. The words poured out of me, somehow finding expression and structure on the page instead of whirling around my head like a tornado or crashing into my breaking heart. Those words became the seed for this book. The priest who came the night Boy died and who conducted JP's funeral with such dignity and respect came to the anniversary ceremony, and he read a psalm and said a prayer. I read what I had written. And then David read a poem written by one of his dearest friends, Frances. The poem recalls a walk Frances and Boy had taken together to the old Murraysburg rubbish dump on the outskirts of the town:

Boy remembered
A solemn little fellow
trudging ahead with proprietary pride
to the old midden at Murraysburg

Nine or ten and childhood chubby
bronze face flushed pink
thick thatch shorn short
and faraway sloe eyes

Heat swelled as the sun took hold
the afternoon insects were out
jagged agaves sliced their way from the stony clay
like leathery dragons

He spoke gravely
smiling slyly
at my id-directed gambit
and bid me follow the dusty distance
I with paraphernalian profusion and he with spade
looking for old bottles and vintage junk
retreating to smoke or shade
and desultory discussion
of the vegetable and the animal
and speculations on the nature of naughtiness
the inconvenient predictability of parents
and the downright peskiness of sisters

But we had come too late
finding only shards
a mix of coloured fragments
in the wake of progress
homogenised
human footprint sterilised

We schlepped back hot and empty-handed
but archetypally satisfied
via Oom Paul's ice-cream emporium
(feeling conspicuously white)
and swam in the backyard dam
– *Frances Hardie, Cape Town, 2012*

A friend spoke. Viv's sons were friends of Boy's and so was she. She remembered how JP used to get into her car after school and she'd ask, 'How are you?' and Boy would say, 'Fine' and then she'd ask, 'How was school?' and she'd get another 'Fine'. If she would ask, 'What did you do?' Boy would say, 'Nothing' and that's about all she could get out of him. One day, after many 'Fine' responses, she tried to trick him and asked, 'What colour is the sky?' He thought a moment and said, 'Blue'. Then he paused and added, 'With clouds'. I loved that. It's so John Peter.

And Blessed sang the song she had sung for us at his funeral. She filled the space with her presence, but her voice was modulated and gentle in that small space underneath our stoep, as opposed to last year at the funeral when it had filled the church. Then we moved upstairs to eat and to just be together. I know that each year these ceremonies and rituals will become smaller, more contained, and fewer people will be there, and that is as it should be. Just as he becomes less physically present in terms of his room, his clothes, his books, his friends – and enters into our memories and our hearts, where one day he will dwell without pain or longing, as just our Boy.

28

In 2004, when I was pregnant with Ruby-Rose, I went for a scan with all three children and John Peter so hoped it was a boy. I remember the gynae saying to me, 'It's a girl', and I looked up at John Peter and caught a glimpse of disappointment cross his face. But it was just a moment and then it was gone. And then he got excited about his baby sister. When I gave birth, all the children were in the room and they watched their baby sister enter the world. John Peter was eight years old. And he held that precious little bundle in his young boy arms and looked at her with such love. He was never very good at changing her nappy, but he tried nevertheless. He bathed her, he played with her, he dressed her, he pushed her in her pram, he had endless patience with her. As she grew up they stayed close, although they were eight years apart. He would lie on the couch with her and watch videos, he played computer games and hide and seek with her, he would give her frights, they would fight, she would bug him and he would bug her.

He loved looking after her. He was her playmate and almost constant companion. She would wake him up early in the morning when the rest of us wanted to sleep, and he would always get up and have time for her and occupy her and play with her. A few days before he died they were playing school-school and we kept his sums on her little blackboard for months after he died. During one of their games earlier in the year he had written in Ruby's diary: 'Today school was fun. I did all my homework, got into trouble for nothing. I am sad now.'

One day after Boy died I found Ruby crying on the bed. She was sobbing her little heart out, saying, 'It's all my fault, it's all my fault that he's dead'. I remember how I held her little body close and I got so angry with Boy. I was thinking: *I will cope, David will cope, even Laine and Annie will survive this – but this little girl – how could he have done this to her – how could he have?* My heart broke wide open at the sadness of it all and the wonder at who we will become because of this and how our lives are so changed. And I said, 'Ruby, what Boy did is nobody's fault and no one is to blame.' But she wouldn't listen to me; she just kept saying, 'It's my fault'. I asked, 'Why do you think it's your fault, Ruby?' and she said, 'Because I used to bug him and irritate him and he used to say to me that I'd be sorry because one day I'd wake up and he'd be dead'. So the only person he trusted with what he was feeling inside was Ruby. And I couldn't take those words away. All I could do was repeat, 'It's not your fault'. Then I said to her, 'It can't be your fault, because it's actually my fault because I was at work that day and didn't come home. No, it's not my fault either, it's Laine's fault because she went off to work in the afternoon. No, no, no, I have it all wrong, it's your father's fault because he left the house to get his hair cut. Or perhaps it's Annie's fault because she was in her room watching a video. Maybe Fikile is to blame because she was ironing.' And Ruby looked up at me and smiled.

I had little awareness of the care my friends were taking over Ruby during the early days after Boy's death. When she spent time at my friend Hedwig's house, Hedwig wrote down the things that Ruby said she loved about her big brother:

What I love about my big brother

1. He is the only one in my family who played with me.
2. He is the only one who really cared for me.
3. He would play teacher-teacher with me and I can remember him from photographs and from my blackboard.

4. He would play lots and lots of fun games with me.
5. He would walk with me to the shops.
6. He would ride his bike and go and buy me things like chips or chocolate or Coke from the shop when I did not feel like walking.
7. He would play with me every single day when he came from school and on weekends.

UNTIL NOW

8. My mom and dad have now freaked out and Annie and Laine have also freaked out, and I am really sad.
9. I wish he had never got hanged up. Died. It makes me really sad and next time I am upset I will tell Mrs Vosters because I am in her class and I love her really much because Boy was in her school and my other school.
10. I wish he had never done that, and then he could be my big brother and he could look like my grandpa if he was old.
11. I wish he was still alive so he could see my new toys and outfit.

JP was always by Ruby's side and now he's gone. I cannot begin to imagine what happens to a six-year-old when she wakes up from her afternoon nap to find her brother dead. All I can do is keep talking to her and reading to her. I was blessed by two stories especially written for Ruby by my friends Vanessa and Patricia. For a long time she was full of fear, but this is diminishing. She wouldn't go to the bathroom on her own. Or to her room. She still doesn't want to be on her own. She has experienced sightings – from where? The other side? On his fifteenth birthday she said she saw him in the kitchen. One evening she ran into the bathroom on her own – she was playing with clay with her friends and wanted to wash her hands. She must have forgotten in her delight and distraction that she doesn't like to go in there on her own. She started washing her hands and then saw something and came running out beside herself – she was nearly hysterical, her heart beating so fast I could see it. I took her back into the bathroom and finished washing her hands and said to her, 'You need to make friends with these things you are seeing'. I sounded sane and rational, but I was disturbed.

It got so bad that I took Ruby to a woman who was recommended to me to do a bodywork session – a woman who is an intuitive. She told me that because of the enormity of our grief dark spirits have entered our house and it needed to be cleansed. Of course this freaked me out even more. I phoned a few people who were recommended to do the cleansing, but I couldn't afford the prices they quoted! Eventually I spoke to another friend and he suggested that we go see Swarmiji, a psychic, at the nearby ashram – we had been to see her about Boy, and she does cleansings and can do them without being present. So off Ruby and I went. Swarmiji was, as usual, all light and glowing and beautiful in her orange robes and full of laughter. She spoke to Ruby about seeing things and her experience as a little girl. She took Ruby seriously and told her to eat well and put on some weight because that would protect her and help her build some strength against these sightings. She also said to Ruby that when she saw them she should just tell them to go away – that they can't harm her, they are just energy. Swarmiji told me that the house didn't need to be cleansed by an outsider – anything that needed to be cleansed could be done by us, as it was our energy that we had brought into the space. It all seemed to make so much sense. Swarmiji told Ruby to start dancing lessons – that she needed to dance. So Ruby is dancing, and she hasn't had a sighting since. She still doesn't want to go into rooms on her own, but she is so much better.

We moved Ruby to a new school at the end of Grade 1, and I had great anxiety about that – me, who would move my children at the drop of a hat, not holding much store or having much faith in schools or the system. But this time, I didn't want to do the wrong thing, I didn't want to be careless – I wanted to make sure the choice was right for Ruby. But how does one ever know this? Eventually I decided that if I was comfortable enough to be involved in the school, Ruby would benefit regardless. So I moved her to a very small new alternative to the mainstream school – operating from a house in the area – where she would get individual attention and a more holistic and integrated education. And every morning Ruby and I go to a nearby park where the kids play before walking down to the school – and she loves it and can't wait to get there each day.

She started having tummy aches in the first term. Then one day she asked me if she could tell the school what had happened to her brother. They light a candle in the mornings and have a sharing or check-in. She asked if I would see if it was okay with the teachers. Of course I knew it would be. And so she told her school friends what had happened and for a while her sore tummy disappeared. But the road with Ruby is not going to be an easy one. Just as she recovers from the tummy aches or the headaches, another challenge emerges. At the moment it is spelling tests and her great anxiety about them. All week she expresses anxiety about the Friday spelling test, even though she usually gets full marks. She tells me, 'I am anxious. I can't help it, I was born this way.' I gently suggest that the anxiety came about since her brother died and I ask her the colour and shape and feeling of it. And she can tell me, most articulately, that the colour is blue and sometimes red and it's a ball and sometimes a star with pointy ends and the feeling is fear and anger. Recently she has started begging to be home-schooled – that I must get a tutor to teach her. She says she wants to stay at home – she doesn't want to go to school – the children don't like her – they just pretend. She has also started telling her teachers that she has very big problems, usually when the tasks at school become challenging. But I am confident that they are equipped to deal with her compassionately and kindly and yet will keep her going, trying, attempting, and not just letting her give up and go the easy route. Her last school report said that she has the emotional intelligence of an adult. I have found a wonderful woman down the road who does body-alignment work and Ruby has had a few sessions. When the struggle gets too much, I make an appointment. And for now that's all I can do. It's not just a day-by-day challenge – sometimes it seems like it's moment by moment.

Ruby's wanting to be home-schooled echoes the pleas of my son: 'I want to stay at home… I want to be home-schooled… Can you get me a tutor? … Why do I have to go to school?' Did Ruby ever hear him say these words – and if so, did she know what they meant at the time? I opened this door for JP and Annie, but I am not opening it for Ruby – but perhaps sending her to her little home-school environment has already done that. Or does she know, as Annie and JP knew, that this is one of my weaknesses? I want to protect them and put them in an environment where they will flourish – I don't believe in the institutions, the uniforms, what seems like senseless learning by rote out of context and with no meaning. I saw how my boy struggled – sitting in a classroom with a teacher telling him stuff when he needed to be learning in an experiential way, by doing. I also learn by doing – well, I learn much easier that way. And after I had tried everything with JP – everything available – I more or less gave up and surrendered to what was close and convenient and affordable. Effectively I said to Boy, 'Just make the most of it. We know what it's about, but it's what we have and where you guys are going.' And within fifteen months JP was dead and a month later Annie had also left the school. It's as if I forgot that Boy needed to be protected. When he was little that was so clear, but as he became a teenager and learnt how to answer back and developed some attitude, he appeared stronger, more resilient. But he wasn't – he was still that introverted, uncomfortable, sensitive boy – and there are days I feel like I abandoned him to a system that didn't serve him, that could never serve him. As if I sort of put him out for the wolves.

I want to protect Ruby from the blunt enquiries of inquisitive children who badger and bully her and want her to tell the story of what happened to her brother. But I can't. All I can tell her is that she doesn't have to share if she doesn't feel safe. The wolves are there. I must give her strength to combat them. That's what I've learnt: don't move on, don't turn away, face it. Whatever it is.

29

What about Boy's other sisters? There's Annie, my dear hypersensitive middle child (for she was the middle child for years before Ruby was born and now is again) with such a thin skin between her and the rest of the world. So attuned to every social nuance and injustice perceived or otherwise, so defensive and aggressive, so empathetic and kind. Always beautifully dressed and groomed – well turned out is our Annie. Yet, while she looks demure and soft, she has a sharp tongue and a quick wit and at times a mouth like a sailor and an attitude to match. But she is softer now. Protective of the underdog, dismissive of the top dog. Just as she starts a good relationship with her brother, and is proud of him, and watches him grow up and become a handsome cool teenager, and has plans to take him on his first jol, out of the blue he goes and hangs himself and she has to be the one who finds him. She protected him when he was alive and she says she is still protecting him, and his honour. What image does she have in her mind for the rest of her life and what is she going to do with it? How will she ever find meaning in what has happened and what she has to live with? She is trying and fumbling and stumbling and picking herself up like the rest of us. In the January after her brother died, she moved to the Cape to start her matric year again. It was a very brave move to make. Her older sister joined her to take care of her, and so on one level the family continued to fracture and fall apart. On another level the girls are both growing strong and independent and are learning how to take their place in the world and how to meet me as their counterpart and friend. There were times when I wished they were with me, and then I'm relieved they were not because I did not have the emotional resources – or any resources for that matter – to deal with them. And sometimes a small dark voice in the back of my mind or deep in a recess of my soul whispers very softly, 'Perhaps they are better off without you.'

Annie is at risk of self-destructive behaviour – she was before her brother died – and I'm sure she is even more vulnerable now. The school she attended for her matric year was small with lots of one-on-one attention and she did so incredibly well in her exams. She is seeing a therapist whom she thinks the world of and this does seem to help. We are all thrilled with her results. I still worry but I have no choice but to let go, let her know that I love her, and that I am here when she needs me. She has a strong will to live. She'll be okay.

Annie and her father share a particular traumatic aspect of John Peter's death: they are left with the image of son and brother hanged by his own hand forever burnt into their souls. It is theirs, something I can never share with them. But it has been beautiful to watch how close his death has brought the two of them. They have developed such a special and unique bond.

And there is my big girl Laine – so clever, so emotionally wise. I asked her once if she thought her parents' various separations and divorce and remarriage had damaged JP. It was a difficult question to ask because I wasn't sure I wanted to hear the answer. But I had to ask her, as a child of this family, how who I am had affected them and her brother in particular. She thought for a long time and then said about the divorce: 'I was seven, so already formed, and I had a lovely life in McGregor. I was fine about it. Annie was five, and JP was two, turning three. He didn't really know what was going on. It's Annie, if anyone, who was damaged by it.' That's all she had to say. Laine was the one who phoned me at work on the Monday before JP hanged himself – he died on the Thursday – and said, 'Mom, somebody has to do something about Boy. He cannot continue like this – he is smoking too much dagga.' And I said to Laine, 'What must I do? Really, what must I do? I am at work all day.' She said, 'I know, Mom. But he needs a firm hand. He needs to be grounded, all his money taken away, his cellphone taken away. He needs to be watched twenty-four hours a day, and he needs to be punished if he's found to be smoking.' And I said, 'How, Laine? In this family, how? With your father and me as parents, how can we do this? We are not policemen. I am at work.' And she said, 'I don't know, but something needs to be done.'

I did hear her. And that's why I was up so early Tuesday, Wednesday and Thursday mornings, pondering the problem. *What's to be done? What can I do? Where can he go?* Interesting that – always looking somewhere else, as though a solution could be found somewhere 'out there'. Although I heard Laine, I also assumed she was exaggerating. Surely if he was smoking so much dagga David or I would smell it – see that he was stoned. And that's why the alarm bells went off that Thursday morning, when I thought, *Maybe it's not dagga…*

After Boy died Laine got depressed. I suppose we all move in and out of a deep sadness and inertia in our own particular ways. Laine directed the school play for RAPS, the annual one-act play festival for schools, and she won best director. She was appointed as assistant director of another play at the Market Theatre with a visiting writer/director. She wrote matric and got four As. But when she wasn't working she was in her bed watching videos until two or three in the morning, and eating. She put on weight after her brother died – over ten kilograms – and I worried about her because how does the cycle of feeling bad, not being able to get out of bed, and then overeating stop? I think it got worse when she moved to Strand with Annie, because she had no friends there, and of course without her Johannesburg contacts and network she had no work. She wants to be a high school teacher and is now at Rhodes University in Grahamstown with the clear intention of getting her BA and then her teaching qualification. She has chosen a university far from all of us so that she can take the time to learn to care for herself and her own needs, instead of caring for and worrying about us. Laine has begun her own journey of healing and has lost weight.

All three girls are straightforward, intelligent, kind and compassionate. The death of their brother has shown them a different way, a gentler path. They have matured beyond their years. They know the very worst can happen and does happen. They are able to intuit someone being fake or false from a mile off. They avoid situations where they can't be themselves. They are Herculean in their inner strength and power.

30

There are questions, so many questions, that I will never have answers for. The only way to find peace is through acceptance – in my heart and soul, not in my rational mind. And I am quite frantic in my efforts to get to the point of this acceptance, misguided as I am in thinking I am going to move from point A to point B in some sort of linear progression. Acceptance is going to be a lifetime coming and it will come and it will go and it's not going to be comfortable and safe and linear. Although I go to therapy and attend groups and talk and talk and talk, I have also found another place I can go to, a place where no words are necessary and yet where healing, and at times profound shifts in consciousness, take place. It is a place where I get in touch with and enter my creative self. I feel useless at times. My brain doesn't put things together quickly and easily anymore. Sometimes I can't concentrate or focus, and I have to force myself to take an interest in films, theatre, exhibitions, dinner parties, gardening, shopping or walking the dogs. But when I make the effort to create something, I can feel my power and strength gently rising and flowing back towards me. It's a tenuous thread, but it's there and at times it's a lifeline. My creativity can't be judged, it's not good or bad, it's not professional or psychological, it's not done to uncover a profound truth or insight, it's simply done for its sake and its sake alone.

It's mine and it's something nobody can take away. And it's about the process, not even the finished product. It comes from a source that doesn't seem to dry up or abandon me. It's always there for me to tap into. It helps build my self-confidence. I love the act of transformation – school socks become the wings of an eagle, a piece of wood gets turned into a bowl, a lump of clay becomes a pot, old clothes and cloth become rag dolls...

I sewed an eagle – it took a year. I sent a photo and wrote a short piece about it for the Compassionate Friends newsletter:

> I am using my son's duvet cover as the background and his old clothes to form the image. I love the idea of transforming his old grey school socks (he didn't like school) into the wings of an eagle. As I stand stitching each piece on by hand, I remember him... it's time for me to be with my son, to sew my memories with each piece of material that used to be a piece of his clothing, transforming them into a soaring eagle. An educational psychologist who assessed him many years ago remembered that when she had asked him what animal he most wanted to be, he answered, 'An eagle'. The reason was simple: 'It can fly, see things from a distance and is completely free,' he said. I don't cry when I sew, my heart doesn't break or ache, I don't feel like I'm suffocating, I don't panic, I don't feel like I'm losing my mind. The creative act of transforming one object (of such pain) into another (of joy and freedom) eases the confined space I occupy most of the time. Sewing the eagle is my alchemy – I am making my type of gold...

I cut up and transform each garment into a wing, the sun shining on the tip of a wing, the leaves dancing in the breeze, the water rippling below, the beak, the eyes, the claws. Each garment is a part of him, something he wore, something he slept on, something that used to sit close to his body. I can remember buying the T-shirts for his fourteenth birthday and wrapping them up and sending them down to McGregor so he would have a present from us on his birthday. And his green tie-dyed T-shirts – I remember how he came to me one early December and asked if he could dye shirts to give to his sisters and cousins for Christmas. I got the T-shirts and the dye and string and we spent a happy day making different patterns and dyeing different-coloured T-shirts and he kept a good few for himself. I cut up his pyjama pants and remember how just before he went down to the Cape for the December holidays – a few months before he died – I was helping him pack and realised he had outgrown all his clothes. The two of us went on a big shop. He was easy to shop with and for. He had a sense of style and an idea of how his jeans should fit and sit, but his tastes were also simple. I cut and I pin and I stitch each leaf and feather by hand. I thread the needle, I sew, I knot, I cut the thread. It is slow, it takes time. I am stitching in my memories of him. Weaving him into every stitch. Each thread a different story of him, of me, as I create something new from what has been. More than anything the eagle has come to represent the before and the now and the transformation. Some days I stitch down many leaves and feathers and some days it's just one and some days it's none at all. But it's there and it's exciting in a low-key kind of way to see it slowly take on the permanence of shape and form and colour and eagle beauty and energy.

The eagle has become our totem for JP – our magical and mythical reminder of him.

I attend a four-day art therapy workshop. It's my first group environment with 'ordinary' as opposed to 'bereaved' people. I am unsure whether I will or should share JP's story as I don't want to overwhelm or for that matter undermine the experience for the other group members. I don't want my story to take over. But by day two I realise I am not going to be able to contribute in any meaningful way if I don't share. It is as if I can't find my voice unless I tell my story. The facilitator asks us to bring a precious object and so I bring JP's eagle. I share my story – contained and truncated. I know it's a *big* story. A powerful story. A mind-blowing story. A story that's difficult to get your head around. The facilitator suggests that we go find a place and create something in response to our special objects. I paint his eagle on large brown pieces of paper stuck together with masking tape, all the while thinking that I want this eagle to be all eagle. I want it to fly and to soar and to glide. I don't want to just represent the eagle – I want my painting to become the eagle. And I love the finished product. It is all eagle.

The next day the group members share the impact my story of Boy has had on them. One woman wears a T-shirt with an eagle on it in honour of JP and says she wants me to know she will never forget him. A dancer says he will choreograph a dance of an eagle. And others are also visibly moved. On the final day we all set up our work and speak to it. I have made a garden, a magical tree, a doll and the eagle. Putting together my 'pieces', I find within myself a long-forgotten enthusiasm and joy for the creative process. I have moments when I feel like a child – not worried about the outcome, just totally lost in cutting and pasting and threading and trusting the process. It feels invigorating to be creating without any pressure or worry about how what I am creating is supposed to look. I share with the group and get feedback, and I am amazed and touched at how JP's story has moved everyone so deeply – and not in a dramatic and overwhelming way, just in a real and responsive way. It is as if I have given them a gift. I am pleased with myself that I have the courage to share it.

A week or so before Boy's sixteenth birthday, Ruby-Rose asks me, 'Why don't you make a boy rag doll for John Peter's birthday?' 'What a totally brilliant idea,' I tell her.

I make rag dolls with Ruby's help, or rather her input. It started when she asked me to buy her a scary monster doll – and who knows where that came from? I said to her, 'Let's make one, and it can be just what you want it to be.' So I drew it, and then I cut the pattern pieces and found some suitable fabric – it was grey – for a monster doll. I made the body and then we went to town. Purple, black and green hair, a black eye and a pink eye, eyes and nose pierced with safety pins, a startling black scar across the cheek, a pierced belly button and a really funky outfit. Then Ruby's friend asked for one and I made it, and then all her little friends wanted one, as did my daughters and my friends' children, and so I've just kept making them. Each one now has a red heart appliqued on it

– the heart is from one of Boy's T-shirts – and so each rag doll gets sent into the world like a little ship of love. Therapeutic to make and loving to send out – just a little gesture of love, giving back.

Some of the rag dolls I make have evolved into approximations of the person they are going to be given to, so they become smaller versions of their owners. I made one for Laine and one for Annie, and Laine's has long wavy hair and rosy cheeks and an outfit that reminds me of her. Annie's has long red hair and a miniskirt. And then I decided to make something that resembles John Peter using the scraps that are left. The hair is tricky because I don't have dark brown wool and for as long as possible I want to make 'rag' dolls and not have to buy fabric, wool, buttons or accessories. So Ruby suggests orange hair. The body is made from JP's duvet cover, and I make a T-shirt from one of his old shirts and applique onto the front of it an image of a skull, also from one of his T-shirts. The doll gets a long-sleeved black jacket from an old hoody. And we make a black beanie for its head that comes right down to his eyes – typical gangsta – that's how Ruby said he wore his beanies. And the doll gets long black pants and grey shoes from Boy's old school socks and some bright yellow shoelaces. From Boy's old tie-dyed T-shirt I make a tie for the doll's wrist, and Ruby searches for accessories that suggest 'weed', as she calls it. And so the doll gets a bracelet on the other arm with black, red, yellow and green beads, and a dagga leaf earring, and a dagga pendant round its neck. And we finish off the doll with a bright yellow scarf made from an old beanie, big dark button eyes and a red heart. And we all love it – my birthday gift from Boy to Ruby.

I sent a photo of Ruby with Boy's rag doll for the Compassionate Friends newsletter with these words:

> The making of rag dolls started about six months after my son, John Peter, died. Ruby-Rose, my youngest daughter, asked me to buy her a scary doll and I suggested we make one. Her friends saw it and they asked me to make for them as well. And so the creating of rag dolls began. Each one gets a red heart stitched to the body from a red T-shirt of John Peter's. I make the dolls and send them

> out into the world with love. I meant to photograph each one that comes into being but I forget and it doesn't really matter... These rag dolls are my thank-you to all the people who brought food... flowers... wine... cigarettes... It's for those who sat with us by the fire through that first winter of our loss... who played with Ruby-Rose and gave time to Laine and Annie (my older daughters)... who listened... cried... gave music... sent photographs and film clips... who gave words... books... hugs... love... poetry... walks... who fetched me and took me to yoga... for those who were just quietly present... for those silent ones who lit candles and gave prayers... They may never get a doll but someone else will... The rag dolls have become my way to give back and give thanks to everyone who has touched me in some way over the past eighteen months... For John Peter's sixteenth birthday on 19 June this year, dear Ruby-Rose asked me to make him a birthday present of a 'boy' rag doll. What a beautiful idea, I thought. And so John Peter's doll was birthed from the scraps of clothes left behind and Ruby-Rose helped decide on the outfit and the accessories. His body is made from his duvet cover. His shoes from old school socks. The laces from his shoes. The 'beanie' from his hoody. The scarf from his 'beanie'... Ruby-Rose loves this doll made especially for her brother, and it's such a comfort being able to refer to John Peter's doll... John Peter Shand Butler was born on 19.6.1996 and chose to end his life on 31.3.2011, when Ruby-Rose was six years old. He was her constant companion and she misses the 'fun' they had together.

I have a yearning to make pots, to work with clay, to repetitively and meditatively pinch the clay. Nina and Paul have been potters in McGregor for many years. I have always admired and appreciated their work, but it seemed so scientific and complicated – the glazes, earthenware, porcelain, bisque firing, salt glazing, oxidisation, wood-firing, and so on. But since Boy died I am suddenly very interested. I want to know and understand the basics and I find that I am able to concentrate long enough to comprehend the basic science behind transforming clay to ceramic. I want to go to the river and find my clay and come home and pinch my pots and light a fire and fire the pots – like an ancient ritual. Like an alchemist magically transforming a lump of clay into a beautiful object. I have an urge to make vessels as if these pots can contain me and what has happened. Earth and fire and water and patient pinching. Ruby and I sit on the back stoep. She makes clay wonderlands with houses and people and rivers and mountains and I pinch my little containers. I attend a few workshops in McGregor with Paul and Nina and meet beautiful people who dedicate their lives to making beautiful pots. And I want to spend the rest of my life creating handmade wood-fired pots.

About five months after John Peter died I went on a journaling retreat – which was probably too soon, but the opportunity presented itself and I grabbed desperately at whatever was on offer. Anything to get me in touch with my centre, anything that had the potential to give me clarity. The journaling was difficult and I think I only managed to touch on the exercises in the most superficial way. To go too deep would have been too hard, too threatening, and my psyche had ways of protecting itself. But the setting was a quiet Christian retreat centre, and we had a marvellous facilitator. It turned out to be a very private, personal experience, and that suited me. After doing individual writing exercises on our own, we would come together as a group to check in and then move back into our own space for the next exercise.

It was during that weekend that I dreamt about my son for the first time after his death. And it was a terrifying dream – a scream from the deepest, most buried, fearful part of myself.

I am walking down a road in a village – it feels like an Irish village, so it's familiar but not known – and somebody tells me that John Peter is being cared for by other people. It is explained to me that he needs to be cared for because he doesn't have all his senses about him. He doesn't recognise people, he doesn't talk, he doesn't respond, he doesn't know who he is, he doesn't know who anyone is. In response I shout and scream that *we* should be taking care of him – why is somebody else taking care of him? How did this happen? I don't understand. He's my son, I love him, I want to care for him. I am told that it will be too distressing for me to be with him in this state and that they are only trying to protect me. I run down the road of the village screaming *I want my son*. I don't care that he doesn't know who I am. I want my son, I want to care for my son. I woke up sobbing and disorientated, with a part of me thinking that he's still alive. As I became fully conscious reality sank in – John Peter is dead.

The facilitator from the journaling retreat, Astrid, thought the dream was very important. She suggested it may have something to do with the pain of realising how unreachable John Peter was – and my fear going forward is that I won't be able to find a way to connect with him. I said I would discuss the dream with my therapist. I wonder if I had been in therapy and/or was doing my morning pages at the time Boy died – if I'd had some way of bringing to the surface my fears and concerns about JP – whether I would have been closer to my instincts and better able to respond to them. Instead I effectively pushed those fears and concerns aside. If I had told a therapist that my son had said, 'Something big is going to happen', would she have said, 'This is serious – perhaps do this or that – try to find out what's beneath the statement' and so on? But this line of thinking doesn't help me now except as a way to move forward – to be more in touch, to reflect more in a disciplined and meaningful way (not just in my head), to be aware and present and listen to my heart and my instinct, and not just drift in a daydreaming sort of way.

One of the exercises on the retreat was to choose a picture from a selection of about thirty images and to go and reflect on it and then write a response to the picture in terms of how it made you feel. Then, after writing, we were to sit quietly again and reflect on the image and see if there was a shift in our feelings. This exercise was quite magical. I chose a picture of a young boy with pad and pen sitting under a large tree in a dappled forest. I was obviously drawn to it because of JP – it spoke to me of loss and what could have been and what was and regret and yearning and aching. After writing I looked at the photo again and my feelings towards the photo had indeed changed, shifting to compassion and empathy for John Peter. For a moment I wasn't just thinking about my loss but was able to connect with what it must have been like to be JP. I want to do more work like this journaling retreat. It is so helpful in terms of developing self-understanding, compassion and empathy.

I read an article in the *Mail & Guardian* – in fact, it's stuck up on the wall next to my desk at work: 'On the pain of death: art in troubled times'. The article includes a photograph of the sculpture *Grieving Parents* by Käthe Kollowitz, a German woman whose son was killed in action during World War I. The sculpture is of a couple set in concrete on plinths: the father is kneeling upright and holding himself stiffly, and the mother is kneeling forward with her arms crossed on her chest as though her grief will overwhelm her. When I look at the picture, I think I feel more like the father, holding myself stiffly frozen, trying to keep myself together. My mother observes that although they are separate in their grief, they are still together and kneeling side by side. Perhaps one day I will create my own sculpture to express something about my own experience of grief and loss.

31

I long for dreams of John Peter. I have had so few of them. And except for the moment during the funeral at the church, I've had no John Peter afterlife experiences. His visit to me in the church let me know that wherever he is, he is happy, and I am grateful for that. I do not know where we go when we die, but I am certain that our consciousness does not disappear. I also believe that I am on this earth leading my earthly existence and those who have died are now in another realm and we are in the places where we are meant to be. But other people have connected with John Peter since his death. I have received so many messages in this regard, some from people I hardly know and some from people I don't know at all. It is as though John Peter's spirit was finding every entry point to us and hoping the message would come through. Because the message was always the same: *I didn't mean to do it and I'm okay*. He visited Annie and David – in fact, he still visits David. The most evocative of these visits took place soon after we returned to Johannesburg from McGregor after burying John Peter's ashes.

Early one morning, David, Annie and I were having coffee on our stoep. David had an appointment with a therapist later in the day and I thought it might be a good idea for him to take something of John Peter with him. We spoke about the reference to the eagle in the email from the educational psychologist, and I suggested to David that he print the email and take it with him. Then we remembered the eagle belt buckle that JP had put aside with his running-away stuff. David went to fetch it. We spoke about the symbolic value of the eagle for Boy, and I remembered the bird's-eye-view drawing he had done of the boat. I got up and went inside to fetch the drawing, and as I did this Annie looked up and said to her father, 'What the fuck kind of bird is that?' David got up and walked into the garden and stood there as a young eagle soared above him and over the house and disappeared into the distance. There are no eagles in Greenside, ever. Was it JP coming past to say, 'Hi guys, I'm okay'?

David, Laine and I went to see Swarmiji at the ashram up the road. She does bereavement counselling under particular circumstances, usually the traumatic death of a child. We sat down, and immediately, without any ceremony or lighting of candles or smudging or chanting, Swarmiji connected with Boy and started laughing. She told us that Boy is very funny and he was making jokes. 'What a great sense of humour he has,' she said. But it is only when she said, 'What's this about shoes? Why is he talking about shoes?' that I really sat up and started paying attention. I said, 'Oh my goodness, we collected his bronzed takkies yesterday.' Swarmiji told us that JP's previous lives had been very exciting and adventurous and that his latest incarnation just didn't quite match up. She said that he found this incarnation a bit boring and that he couldn't find anything to get excited about. She said that his existence simply didn't make sense for him this time around. 'But,' she said, 'he is making up for it now and he is having the time of his life out there.' She told us that he is learning lots of interesting stuff and that he is excited and motivated and wants us to know that he is really happy. She said it is ridiculous that JP is having such a good time in his realm and we are so miserable down here. She told us that he looks a bit like James Dean in his denim jeans and white T-shirt, and that he looks older than his fourteen years and very handsome.

She asked us if we had any questions for him and I asked if

something had happened to him at boarding school. She said, 'Yes, something happened to him there, but he doesn't want to talk about it.' I ask if JP had a message for Annie, and Swarmiji said, 'Yes, tell her not to share all my secrets!' Swarmiji also asked which one of the sisters is wearing Boy's T-shirts (Annie is) because he says it is fine that they wear his clothes but it's not very flattering. I find it a comforting visit, and not so much because Swarmiji is able to connect with Boy – in fact, I find it very jarring to have someone sitting in front of me who can see and chat to my son and I am left with that person's interpretation or translation of him and what he's saying. As if that person can tell me something I don't already now. I know my son. I know that JP was bored and that nothing excited him much. I don't need a stranger to tell me who my son was. I know he didn't fit in. That he was uncomfortable in his earthly skin. That he didn't understand the point of what most humans get up to. That he preferred his own company. That he didn't need much. That he found life boring. That he wasn't motivated. That he had a great sense of humour. That he is now learning and loving learning because it's experiential. I can imagine that. He's now light and free like he never was on earth. I can imagine that too.

But what is a great comfort is the spiritual perspective Swarmiji gives. I need to hear that he's happy and that all a parent wants is for their children to be happy. My son is happy now. He is in a better place. I'd hoped he would find this better place somewhere on planet Earth but he didn't. He's in a good place and I have to learn to take this into my heart and really accept this. Wherever he is, he is okay. What more do we want for our children? For them to be here, of course, but I don't say that to Swarmiji.

My therapist, Midge, whom I started seeing after Boy died, was told of his death by a mutual friend on the night he died. She is a Reiki master who works with energy levels, and her impressions were that he was struggling with what had happened, that he was confused and didn't understand that he couldn't get back into his body, although he had tried to do so. But eventually he realised that he was dead to the physical world and accepted that and moved on.

David and I went separately to a psychic. David's visit was more profound than mine, but by then she knew our story and I can't help being sceptical. There are charlatans out there, and we are so hopelessly vulnerable when it comes to things we don't understand and when our hearts have been ripped wide open and we need answers and connection. In that vulnerable state we are easy to trick. But it's not about that so much as the fact that the message is only as good as the messenger: John Peter may be hammering away at the messenger trying to say something but may be totally misunderstood. This psychic told us that John Peter was taken away by the souls who were hovering to help him across and they took him away almost immediately to shield and protect him from witnessing our trauma, and they told him they would bring him back later to be with us.

I don't know what to do with all the psychic stuff. What does happen to our consciousness and spirit when we die? I don't doubt that various people can and did connect with my son – I just haven't worked out how useful that is to me here firmly on this earth and of this earth. I have to cope and learn to live with him not being physically present to me now where I find myself. The help I need is to get me through my ordinary earthbound days. And though it's comforting to hear that he is very, very happy, we are not. We want him here, back in the midst of this mad crazy chaotic family, and he's not. There are days when I think the most we can hope for is not to self-destruct entirely.

I went to be blessed by a visiting Buddhist lama – I suppose I was longing for some sort of magical epiphany: *Ah, now I understand.* I waited for a long time sitting by myself on a chair outside his room. It is very seldom that I sit alone without distraction or tasks to occupy me, and when it does happen I get very emotional. The sadness of what has happened grips me and the tears flow and there is nothing I can do to stop them. So by the time I entered the lama's room (trying to remember the rules of engagement – which hand to give him the scarf with and the money and not to turn my back and to bend my knees, and so on) I was sobbing. I told him what had happened, and he said in a compassionate but distant voice, 'Are you a Buddhist?' 'No,' I said, 'although I have read a lot.' And he said, 'It's a pity, because if you were a Buddhist you wouldn't be suffering. Your suffering is pointless. Your suffering is stupid. [Yes, he actually used the word 'stupid'.] Your son is gone from this earth. Your suffering isn't helping anybody – not him, not you, not your family. The only constructive thing you can do is pray – pray to whoever or whatever you want to pray to – that he doesn't have to come back to earth again and repeat earthly suffering. Pray that he is released from samsara.'

32

There are worlds within worlds – realities within reality – and until something calamitous happens we are not aware of this, only of our small safe world. There is a double-storey house in Waverley with a sign on the outside wall that says 'Compassionate Friends'. I had driven on that road hundreds of times but never noticed the sign. Before Boy died, I didn't know this organisation existed. Their purpose is to provide solace to grieving parents. The Compassionate Friends are angels. They phone from time to time as if from nowhere and ask in a gentle voice: 'How are you?' And I don't have to pretend that I'm fine; there's no point. They know because they've been there. And we just chat for a while, and I've been heard and understood – by somebody not trying to tell me that it's not my fault and that I mustn't feel guilty; they know the struggle of entering normal life.

The Friends provide all sorts of groups for all sorts of situations, including a suicide-support group, and I've been to meetings of this group many times. It's not a therapy group like the one I attended at LifeLine – Compassionate Friends is mainly for parents. It's a safe space to share, to listen, to be heard. Listening to other parents' stories has been the most healing. Sometimes I look at my family and the road we have walked together, and I know we are unconventional to say the least. It hasn't been a straight path. There have been many twists and turns, cul-de-sacs, dark corners, sadnesses, heartbreaks, multiple 'separations' (as Laine so euphemistically calls them) and multiple reunions, but also a lot of love and life and adventure and excitement and colour and an abundance of creative energy. Sometimes I think our tragedy resulted from 'the twists and the turns' – that had our lives been straighter, somehow this wouldn't have happened. I wonder whether my open-minded, boundary-less and permissive trust in my own life force to get us all through created a space within which anything is possible. And when I sit in these groups I see such ordinary parents there – and I use the word 'ordinary' with the greatest respect and envy – smartly dressed couples who live in houses with a lounge suite, a flat-screen TV, a manicured lawn and a swimming pool, who have high-achieving children, who are high-achieving adults themselves... until their perfectly constructed lives are swept from under them and they are brought to their knees with the scream of every parent who has lost a child to suicide: 'How can this happen to me?' One mother I remember clearly in her navy suit, her hair highlighted and coiffured, her nails manicured. She had *no idea*. Her son was at university doing well – he'd always done well. He had lots of friends, lots of trophies and medals and certificates. He was her rock, always able to give advice and support. And one day, out of the blue, he killed himself.

Because we can only see ourselves in relation to the other, these other families and their stories bring an objectivity to my story. Suicide can happen to anyone, anywhere, at any time. It can happen even if you are expecting it and are on your guard, even if your child has made previous attempts and is seeing psychologists and psychiatrists and is on medication and is being watched 'like a hawk'. Even with all the love in the world, all the understanding, all the 'right' responses activated, it can still happen. It can happen if your child isn't displaying signs of depression or other mental illness, isn't using drugs. It can happen if your child has a rich and full social life. It can happen if your child is athletic and participates in team sports. It can happen if your child has a passion and actively engages in that passion. It can happen...

Suicide sometimes happens under the most extraordinary circumstances, leaving survivors to wonder, how did he or she get it right? How did that kill them? From a towel rail in a bathroom using a belt? In the bath from the towel rail? Even with my Boy I am left with a sense of ambiguity. Did he really mean it? If he meant it, why that space? There may not have been enough height – he could have been seen or found – the policeman using one hand to undo the knot he tied to the top of the frame – why didn't it give under his weight? I have also heard stories that make one wonder, how did that *not* kill that person? How can you survive walking in front of a truck on a busy highway at night? These are all existential questions – or perhaps questions of God. Even in this darkest of acts, the hands of the gods are still at work. Is it fate, or is it written, that this one will succeed in the attempt and this one won't? Just like any death?

Every month I scour the Compassionate Friends newsletter for the suicides. I am trying to find other parents who have had such a young child kill him- or herself, but I swear Boy is the youngest. There have been one or two sixteen-year-olds but no fourteen-year-olds. It's surreal. One day your life is one way and the next moment it's gone. I now know there is nothing profound or new in this realisation. I am not the first person who has had the unimaginable happen. And what if he had died in a car accident instead? I know there are many of the same questions associated with this kind of sudden death, especially *What could I have done to prevent it?* With hindsight, so many accidents seem as if they could have been avoided. The 'if onlys' are also there. But with suicide there is a difference. A car accident doesn't force such deep introspection and self-doubt and insecurity. I wouldn't keep asking, 'What did I do wrong? How could it have been different? What sort of parent am I that I couldn't protect my son from the ultimate in self-harm? What didn't I see? What signs did I miss?'

One day I am given a magazine article to read. Titled 'Remembering Embeth', the article is about a girl who killed herself when she was thirteen years old. Her parents had suspected depression and she had been on a treatment programme. The parents had responded to the symptoms and had done everything they could to help their daughter, and they were told by the professionals that she would be fine and she wasn't and she killed herself. And just as my story helps other parents feel 'lucky', so this story makes me feel 'lucky'. I am lucky because my son was fourteen years old when he died. How perverse is that?

I hear it and see it time and time again. At a Compassionate Friends meeting a mother of a twenty-something-year-old who shot himself in the head looks at me and says, 'I look at you and I feel so lucky. So lucky that I had more years with him, that I saw him become a man.' And what's even more perverse is that I don't mind what she says. I am relieved that some good can come from JP's death, even if it's to help make another grieving mother feel 'lucky'. At another meeting, a mother shares with me how lucky she feels that she and her husband were home to pull their son's body out of the swimming pool and to be with him. David shares how lucky we were that the ineptitude of our police system ensures we had eight hours with our son's body. Other parents are not so lucky. A mother shares with us that the police wouldn't let her see her son's body because of the damage from the gunshot to the head.

I also attended a suicide-support group at LifeLine. It evolved into more of a therapy group. It was eight sessions long and a closed group, meaning the group members commit to all eight sessions and don't come and go as they wish. (That is the style of the Compassionate Friends support group, which takes place once a month and parents come and go as they please.) This is not a bereavement group for parents, but the participants are all survivors of suicide. (That's another shock. I am now what is termed a 'survivor'.) All the suicides are male and all the participants in the group are women. There were about eight of us at the start of the group, but the core committed group is four: a sister, a wife, a daughter and me, a mother. It seems my story helps give perspective to what the others are going through. It's as if my story helps them cope because they look at me and they can't quite believe what I am going through. It's not because I sit there wailing and weeping and tearing at my clothes, but it's because of a few words: my son died, he hanged himself, he was fourteen years old. And again I get to hear how 'lucky' my story makes someone else feel. It makes the wife feel 'lucky' because her husband is dead, but she still has her two beautiful sons and she doesn't know what she'd do without them. In this seemingly minor but somehow significant way, my pain, my loss, my tragedy does benefit other grieving people.

The group is helpful. It forces me to listen to others and connect with their pain and loss. It gets me out of my head a bit and in touch with my heart and helps me feel related to others. But sometimes it's incredibly challenging. I listen to the daughter of a suicide. She is an adult woman and still crying fifteen months after her old and sick father shot himself. 'How could this have happened?' she asks over and over again. If I had the energy, or if I hadn't already learnt that there is no point in interfering with anyone's grief or telling them what/how/when they should be behaving, I would say to her, 'Stop! Listen to yourself, move on already, get over it. Do you hear me sitting here crying, "This wasn't meant to happen"? And it was my son, he was fourteen, your father was old and sick.' But I don't say any of that; I breathe and I let her cry. And I hope for her that after the final session something has eased for her, and some of the responsibility and blame has dissipated, and her yearning for a different ending is gradually being replaced with acceptance of what is.

In some sessions I find myself talking more about the present than about John Peter – my daughters; David; how things are so very, very different now; my work; my friends; my future. We do my geneogram. A geneogram depicts a family's relatedness, structure and history to reveal the family's emotional geneology. The process in group is a spontaneous one, and the facilitator just starts putting down my family members on a flipchart as I say who married whom and what children were born to whom and mentioning what seems significant in terms of family emotional history, such as who was depressed, who was an alcoholic, who was rebellious, and so on. Warmth, love and acceptance come across strongly in my geneogram. But the most profound theme to come out is the 'absence' of men. Not just physically absent men, but also men who were in the background not making much noise. It's as if JP came at the end of a line of men who lived in the shadow of overpowering, efficient, competent, capable and loud women. The facilitator asks the question, 'Did he carry that?'

33

My mother often says that if you can get teenagers past the age of fifteen relatively intact, they'll be okay. I think she may be right.

I remember Annie and Laine asking after Boy died, 'What good is therapy if it's the soul that's in trouble?' Talking isn't going to help if the soul is sick. Only a healer can help – someone who has the magical ability to heal the soul: an ancient Native American healer, an African traditional healer, a South American shaman, an Aborigine medicine person, a witch, a psychic, a spiritualist…

I read a book about a father, a mother and an autistic son and a horse and a journey to a South American shaman for healing. Could there have been healing for JP – if we had known the depth of his despair? If I had known, if I had listened to my intuition – it was telling me, whispering, yelling, *Something is wrong*. I knew something was wrong; I just didn't know what to do about it. But yes, I did know what to do, I just didn't have the courage to act. I knew school was a waste of time and I wanted to take him out – if I had listened to my heart, I would have taken him out of school. Laine said to me recently, 'He didn't have to go to school. He was never going to go to university, he wasn't going to get an office job – it didn't matter if he went to school or not.' And she is right. It didn't matter and I knew it didn't matter, yet there was the nagging voice of convention saying, 'What will happen to him without an education?' Yet I knew that what he was receiving was not an education – the most I hoped for was socialisation, but he was never going to be socialised, or rather, he was as socialised as he was ever going to become. Yes, school kept him occupied, but it didn't stop him being bored, distracted and mischievous. School did more damage than good. What little life he had left in him was slowly siphoned out of him and then for extra measure was stomped upon: *You think you're a big boy? I'll show you what you are, you little nothing. 'Hey kids, who don't you want in your class next year?' And for good measure let's read out the names of those kids who are not wanted – ah JP, aren't you lucky? You are second least wanted*. What care… what emotional maturity.

Laine said to me, 'Mom, he could have stayed at home forever. Lots of parents have to support children with disabilities for their entire lives. You would have done that for him – if you'd known.' And I said, 'Yes, Laine, I would have done that.' Little does she know it's one of the recurring themes that haunts me: if I had known, he could have stayed at home; if it was so difficult for him in the world, I would have looked after him for as long as I lived. It is a shocking thought, because it shows on some level I understood just how extreme he was, how extreme the situation was. But I didn't trust my intuition. I treated him like my other children. And he wasn't like my other children. If only he'd had something obviously wrong with him, something tangible that could be diagnosed. If only he hadn't coped academically – if only. If instead of sitting by the kitchen window each morning, smoking and worrying and wondering, I had gone and spoken to him as he was waking up – while he was still soft and open, before the harshness of the day had closed him up – I could have crawled in next to him and held him – while he was still sleepy enough not to push me away – and asked him, really asked him, 'What do you need? What can I do for you?' Instead of trying to work it out for myself, I could have just asked him – asked him to write me a letter like he did when he was in Grade 4. I could have said, 'I see you are struggling, that something's up. Write to me and tell me what you need. I will listen.' But by then I'm sure he didn't believe that

I would. And what would he have written to me if I'd asked and he'd accepted the request? *Dear Mom, I don't want to go to school anymore. I hate it there – I hate the teachers – I hate most of the kids – I get teased – I get bullied – I don't know what's going on half the time – I am bored – I hate it. Some days I hate it so much I feel like dying. Please take me out of the school. Please let me be home-schooled at home.* And what would I have done if I'd received a letter like that from him? Allowed him to stay at home? I don't know.

I explained to his therapist (whom he saw for a few months after he came back from boarding school) that I didn't know what to do about him and high school. I told her that he was at the local high school and that he wasn't happy there – that it took a while for me to realise, but it was clear that school was a waste of time. But by then, I said, I had hit a dead end. I had no more energy or money to find an alternative. He had already been to too many schools – at least the local school was nearby and convenient, because on some level I knew that unless there was another Anam Cara, he wouldn't be happy at any school. The therapist concurred. She affirmed: 'He wouldn't have been happy at any school.'

We – all of us – have to learn to listen, to listen not just with our ears, although that would be a good start, but to listen with all of our senses. We don't listen, we don't trust, we don't believe, we don't see, we don't speak. I was given the gift of a special child. It was my responsibility to protect him and I failed. It is only in his death that I can see this. If only it had been more obvious.

Were there just too many children? Was it just too much? I felt so responsible – rightly or wrongly – to keep the show on the road, and I failed. I tried so hard. I loved them all so much. I was juggling so many balls and one dropped. I just wish it wasn't Boy. Why couldn't it have been my work, or me, or anything other than one of my children?

My mother writes:

> And the guilt... This is normal when someone close takes his own life. You are not alone – the boy has two parents. And two

> powerful older sisters. I don't think it was illogical. For John Peter it made perfect sense. I'm slowly beginning to accept that. I can see that to put it into the context of your whole existence is a thrashing about for understanding. But this is about *him* and all the things in the world that influenced and impacted on his life. Maybe his darkness was beyond your/our control. Genetic? Hereditary? Maybe.

A friend told me about a documentary he had recently watched about America and the over-medication of children. He said a teenage boy of about fourteen years of age had been diagnosed with Asperger's syndrome. He said you could hardly identify anything 'wrong', other than that he was a bit of a loner and that he was perhaps slightly off centre, coming from a slightly different angle. The father was being interviewed about his fears for his son and he said he was scared his son might do something like jump out of a window and die. The interviewer asked, 'Why, because you fear he is suicidal?' and the father said, 'No, because I'm scared he could do something that stupid'. And again a light goes on. It resonates. That's my boy. I could be that father. I had a son who I always felt could do something really stupid. And then he did.

I wonder again about observations about my son, and when I speak to Midge about him, she says, 'Your son was on the autism spectrum, of that I have no doubt. You must understand, he was wired differently.' And he was, but it was so slight – such a discreet difference, barely discernible. The school readiness tests picked nothing up. His nursery school picked nothing up. His first primary school picked nothing up. The educational psychologist who spent the day testing him picked nothing up. His therapist in Grade 7 picked nothing up. The drug counsellor picked nothing up. But I always knew that Boy was different and that there was something different about him. I just couldn't put my finger on it. He was introverted. He was sensitive. He wasn't verbally or socially dextrous. He wasn't easy in his skin. He wasn't able to protect himself. It was as if he didn't have self-preservation instincts. He did stupid things. We used to tell him, 'Don't do stupid things because you always get caught.' He didn't even have the guile to do the naughty things and not get caught. How do you survive in the world if you don't know how to? If you don't have dreams for the future? If you take everything at face value? If you do stupid things just because somebody suggests you do them? If you can't respond, do you react instead? It was like there was an emotional vacuum, a disconnect. Did he watch us all operating in the world, communicating, talking, friends coming and going, witty retorts, angry sisters who could fight for their place and their rights, answer people back?

One memory I have of him is how he would laugh inappropriately, especially in a classroom situation. Who told me this – the girls? the teachers? His laughter was a defence when he didn't know how to respond. Or on other occasions, a teacher would ask, 'JP, where is your book?' 'It's at home,' he would answer. And the teacher would think he was being cheeky even though he was just answering the question. He didn't know how to lie, or that it was expected that he should spin a bit of a story and be apologetic.

To be a good mother to John Peter was simply to be present to him and I didn't always succeed in that. He was never going to give me stuff to work with – he was never going to fight or resist. Except the one night when I tried to get his cellphone – the night we knew he was stoned. He didn't want to give it to me. The scramble for the phone got physical. I was trying to grab it from him and he was resisting – until later, when he brought me his phone. Something prompted me to look for the SIM card, and of course he had removed it. Did he eventually give me the SIM card? I can't remember – it's a bit of a blur. I think he must have put it in and deleted all sorts of stuff, and then he gave it to me. And I told him that his phone is in my name and all I had to do was phone Vodacom and request the records and I could find out everything that was on the phone. I said it without really meaning it – or should I say without really believing that this was possible. I still don't know – could I have phoned Vodacom and requested the SMS transcript? I wanted to after he died, when mining the little I had for something, anything, that would give clues to why he did what he did. And after he died I was so filled with guilt that maybe he had believed that this was possible, that I could get the phone records – and that he had something to hide, something that he believed was so bad that he was scared to live with the consequences of me finding out.

When he stole the R800 from me that Wednesday night before he died and was found out, perhaps he thought I was going to go to Vodacom and request the records. I never spoke to him about it again – to tell him that I wouldn't do such a thing, that I didn't even know if it was possible. And I can't help wondering. But it's all second guessing – one of the main black endless tunnels I go down that don't lead anywhere.

I love his corner of the back garden. I often sit down there. The rusty white metal outdoor table and four chairs nestle there among the shrubs that I planted myself and watered and composted and watched grow: the Johannesburg Gold tree, the yellow jasmine, the deep- red ornamental plum, the bloukappie, the elderberry, the bottlebrush. If you look skywards while sitting in that fertile grotto, you see gold and red and green, fine leaves and fat leaves, twigs and branches all overlapping with each other. There are birds – pigeons, grey louries, starlings, Indian mynas, and if you are lucky you may spot a crested barbet – and lizards and geckos and earthworms and butterflies and bees, so many bees. If you look towards the house it stands there solidly: a square white block with a large blue sun-bleached umbrella providing some shade from the white-hot African sun. And the sky is so blue – the deepest, brightest blue against the geometric white lines. The magenta bougainvillea flowers cover the stoep railing and overflow into the back garden, and the jasmine Boy planted twists itself around the stair railing. And there are herbs and vegetables in summer: lots of basil and rocket and spinach, and sometimes garlic and potatoes and Chinese cabbages, and there's the sage that Boy planted and other pungent-smelling herbs from the Karoo that love the Johannesburg climate. The mulberry tree drops its nearly black berries all over the grass. The berries stain our fingers and lips as we pick them and eat them, laughing at the mess we make.

There is also the jungle gym and shelter where Boy used to play when he was younger. We would attach the hose to the top of the slide and the children would climb up the ladder and slide down all afternoon – until there was a swamp at the bottom of the slide.

How often JP sat down there. He must have loved that place. Close to nature, away from the rest of us. And peaceful.

It's difficult for me to speak to the girls about his dagga smoking, mostly because I don't want them to tell me something I don't want to hear. I already feel so responsible, like I didn't take action. Like I let it slip somehow. Like I was neglectful. But Laine, Annie, Boy's cousin Sarah and I did manage to have a good conversation about this difficult topic. I asked them, 'Do you think that the dagga smoking changed him?' In unison Laine and Sarah said yes and my heart sank. Then they started speaking about how it changed him: 'He became less introverted... he came out of his shell... he would talk and laugh and joke, like a normal kid... it released his inhibitions... he would answer back... he would respond.' I asked, 'So you don't think it made him paranoid and delusional? You don't think he heard voices or saw stuff that wasn't there?' And they both said, 'No, not at all.' But then Annie said, 'He was smoking it on his own at the bottom of the garden during those last months and who knows what he saw or heard or felt?' She added, 'People shouldn't smoke dagga on their own. That's when they become paranoid because they don't know what's going on and they have no one to share it with to break the intensity.'

Laine and Annie told me that they have not smoked dagga since JP died and will never smoke again. I got the sense of the three of them together – the girls knowing what was going on and wanting to protect Boy from our punitive anger. They didn't tell us how much he was smoking because of sibling collusion. In the most positive way they didn't want to 'snitch' on him – until that Monday, when Laine realised it was getting out of hand and something had to be done.

They told me about a girl they hung out with in McGregor that last Christmas holiday. They had all gone to sleep in the same room, and the girl was next to Boy. In the morning when they had woken up she was wearing JP's boxer shorts. They all laughed as they told me the story, and I laughed too. I was so happy he had slept next to a girl and had known something of youthful passion. How many other shared teenage adventures do they have? Boy had a life outside of me, his father, his grandmother. As all teenagers do, he led a life that we knew nothing about, in which he was just a regular kid doing regular kid things.

Laine also spoke of his will, giving me another perspective as I go down the tunnel and follow the thread of the boy who didn't seem self-motivated, didn't have an inner will to propel himself forward. She reminded me that he did do stuff on his own. He asked for a car radio and speakers for his birthday – that's all he wanted – and he got them and he built the speaker boxes on his own. He had a little guidance from David, but the project was not motivated by us or even suggested by us. Boy had a picture in his mind and he acted on it. He would visit Thando on his own volition, not because I suggested he should go but because he wanted to. He got David to build the go-kart because he wanted it – again, he had a picture in his mind and followed through on it. The same with his bike rides. The same with going to the shop. I know they seem like insignificant actions – isn't that what everyone does? – but he wasn't like everyone. And he certainly wasn't motivated by getting high marks or winning trophies or being number one. He already knew that stuff didn't hold much real value. It was as though from a young age he knew that winning meant somebody else had to lose. I just wish I could have done more to help him be the very best *he* could be. There is some comfort in knowing I did try – we all did.

The girls also spoke about his crush on their close friend Amy. How intensely did he feel that? There was this gorgeous, easy-going, witty, voluptuous eighteen-year-old in the house all the time – and JP was fourteen years old and all hormones and trying to act cool. Did those feelings he had no control over overwhelm him? The girls said that once when he was drunk he told them that he felt like a twenty-one-year-old trapped in a fourteen-year-old's body and that none of them could imagine how difficult it was for him.

It's true that he was older than his years, as though he had lived a 100 lifetimes and coming back this time was a bit of a bore – as if he knew it all already and where it would lead. He wasn't that interested in this business of life and school and marks and rugby games and careers and jobs and wives and children and work and then death. He took a short cut straight back to the source.

I have read just about every book ever written on suicide – and the phenomenon remains inexplicable. It doesn't matter how or from which perspective, angle, depth it is explored, no one has an answer to why it happens or how to prevent it in an absolute sense. Nothing will change the fact that people kill themselves. All we can be certain of is that we the living can manage how we respond to it – our attitude. But there are insights, glimpses of the truth, that I gain from my reading. This world didn't make much sense to Boy. He didn't feel alive in it; he was a little numb – a little disconnected; he definitely felt anxious. He had eczema on his face, and he tried every cream we could find. I noticed that his hands would also start peeling in a startling way. That first happened when he was in Grade 7 and I said to him, 'It's stress, Boy'. I was aware, but what to do? Lots of kids have eczema – I just watched it come and go and would note it. It didn't cause him any physical discomfort. He just didn't like what it did to his appearance and was self-conscious about it. The eczema did seem to get better those last few months, as he grew up and seemed to become stronger in himself and more assertive – but perhaps that assertiveness came from being stoned.

I remember taking Boy to the bushveld boarding school when he started Grade 6. As I drove away from the school, leaving that eleven-year-old on his own, I just cried and cried and cried. Every cell in my body wanted to turn around and fetch him. *But this is what he wants*, I said to myself. But was it really? How can an eleven-year-old know what he wants? We had driven him out there to look at the school so we could decide if this was the right place for him – he had opted for the bush school after I said home-schooling wasn't a possibility. I remember thinking at the time, where else can I send him? That maybe it would be good for him to be away from his strong, overpowering sisters, and for him to be in the bush, which he so loved, and in a school where he would be in small classes and get one-on-one attention and meet farm kids. I remember wondering how he would know where to go, what to do – he doesn't ask – he doesn't have us to support and protect and guide him. How would he manage? Well, he did manage that first year. He came home most weekends, or we went to visit him. We went camping a few times in the Waterberg. He loved that the most. He built himself a shelter in the bush – a hiding place – and I'm sure he went there to escape, and to imagine he was living by himself in the bush and surviving on his own. His imagination was full of wild animals, and evening fires, and trapping and foraging and providing for his own meals – and just wandering and observing and being part of nature. He showed us a rock outside the boarding house. He said he used to sit there – just sit and watch.

I can't help my wandering mind – it goes back to this time, and before this time. What if I hadn't taken him out of primary school that first time and put him into therapy instead? Sometimes it seems that all we had shown him was that he was strong enough to withstand cruelty and teasing and unkindness. I can't forget his letter begging me to take him out of school. It's not in my nature to leave a child who is suffering in an environment where he is so unhappy he will die if he has to stay there. But what if… that little voice… what if we had shown him that he wouldn't die if he stayed there? But then he wouldn't have had the best year of his life at Anam Cara – and the outcome would probably have been the same, our allotted time on this earth and all that. And how does this little voice, the what-ifs, serve me? Perhaps the little voice can help me now – with Ruby perhaps, as we start the cycle of resisting school and nagging to be home-schooled. I will remember my little voice – and grow her strong. I know that Ruby is not her brother. She is made more of the stuff of her sisters: she is connected, present, expressive; she can protect herself.

That is what is so startling to me about JP as I remember him, as I piece him together with these words. My sense that he was unable to protect himself overrides all other impressions of him. It's as if he had no armour – no quick retorts – no ability to fight back. If his dealer had offered him heroin, he would have said, 'Sure, I'll try that' – with his brain having no way of alerting him to danger. It wasn't even that Boy was risk-seeking – it was that he didn't have the emotional functioning to comprehend that a situation was dangerous, that maybe he shouldn't do whatever was on offer. And that's why we needed to protect him.

When I describe Boy to my therapist and his therapist from his Grade 7 year, they both say that he was on the autism spectrum. Obviously highly functioning autism, because the psycho-educational report didn't pick anything up. And when I read about autism and Asperger's, there are resonances – a-ha moments – but gaps as well. I don't think Boy had Asperger's, but maybe he so disguised it that not even his teachers could pick it up. I often thought he didn't quite know what was going on. But his intellectual functioning was fine according to the tests: his IQ in all fields was above average. It was his emotional functioning that was unusual. And as I write this, I pave the way for my session with his therapist on Friday. I haven't spoken to her since Boy died – he stopped seeing her at the end of Grade 7 – and I am anxious and nervous about what I may hear. Yet I am sure that if she had something revelatory to tell me, she would have contacted me after she heard he had killed himself. So I expect I am likely to hear the familiar.

34

I went to see Boy's therapist; he saw her every two weeks during the fourth term of Grade 7. She commented on my short hair, saying I looked different; I said, 'I am different'. We sat down – hers is a welcoming room, with lots of candles, a clarinet, books piled high, colourful cloths and cushions covering the chairs. On her table was a book on love and relationships by the great guru Osho; I have been reading him of late. She made tea and I sat and waited.

I thought about how Boy used to sit in this room. What did he think while he sat here? Was he anxious? Did he wonder why I sent him here and what he was supposed to do and say during the hour? He always just went – I suppose because I told him he had to. He seldom offered much resistance.

The therapist returned with the tea. I said I was sure she had nothing 'new' to share with me and that if she had she would have contacted me, so I told her I had come so that she could share her memories, insights, impressions of my son during the short time he spent with her. She said yes, she didn't see him for very long and so she didn't have much to offer me. She said he was very closed – he didn't let her in at all. Once or twice she thought she had gained some trust but then he would close down again. She remembered that John Peter was really looking forward to Laine coming back from Argentina and that he was painting Laine's room for her. (He spent days helping me get her room ready for her.) He told her that his best friend was Thando from next door; the therapist said they were obviously very close, as he spoke about Thando a lot. He told the therapist that his little sister could be very irritating. He hated the headmaster at his boarding school in the bushveld. She said he was very unhappy there and didn't want to be there. She said that he had stolen from the headmaster, and it was because he was unhappy there and he hated the man. I reminded her that he had stolen the money from the headmaster's wife.

I asked the therapist, 'Did something happen to him when he was there?' She said yes, she believed something did happen to him there. Boy didn't say that something happened there, but that's what she believed. She asked me what my instincts as a mother told me. I said yes, something happened there. She said I should trust that. But she added that that wouldn't be the only reason he killed himself – it was an accumulation of a lot of stuff – but it would have contributed hugely. She remembered going onto her laptop and Googling the school and asking JP to come show her the school and look at the photos with her. But he refused to look at the photos of the school.

I said, 'His life wasn't that bad, was it?' and she said, 'Yes, it was. For him it was.' He created a fantasy in his mind, like a lot of fourteen- to fifteen-year-olds do – a fantasy that had little bearing on objective reality but became his reality. She said – a few times – that 'The CD had finished and he didn't have the will to change it or to put another one into the CD player'. She said he had been thinking about it for a long time – that it was not an impulsive, spontaneous, unconsidered action. I mentioned to her that I had been told that John Peter was on the autism spectrum. She confirmed that he didn't have the ability to code and decode – that children like Boy can't make sense of the world, don't understand social cues or expectations, can't find meaning the way more 'normal' people do. She said children like Boy learn to mimic behaviour so that they fit in, that they don't have the same emotional cues and tools as we do. I told her that I remembered my desperate tears as we drove away from the boarding school, wondering how in the world he was going to cope and know what to do. The therapist said that he knew what to do because he followed the other boys and copied them – but he didn't know from inside of himself what to do.

She asked me if I believed in the afterlife. I said that I knew he was safe and happy, whatever form or shape his consciousness has now taken. She asked me for details about the day he died, and about how he killed himself. I tell her, once again revisiting his death – remembering that I don't actually know what killed him; I don't have the autopsy report yet. I tell the therapist that I have Googled how people die from hanging: usually they strangle to death and it takes a while and they look disfigured and discoloured and usually there are signs of struggle. I said it was so strange with Boy because he looked like he was sleeping and there were no signs of struggle. She asked if he perhaps broke his neck. I said I didn't know, but that it was highly unlikely because he didn't jump except for what could have been a small jump from Ruby's car seat just to give momentum.

How did it work – physiologically? I want the autopsy report to find out if there were any signs of self-mutilation… any other substances in his body. I think I know the answer – all I will find out is cause of death and that may just be suffocation from hanging or something medical and unhelpful. I still want to know.

The therapist said that Boy was high risk, that for a boy the age of fourteen to fifteen is a high-risk time. I thought hard about this: my son was high risk. I tried to unpack that. What is high risk? Is a high-risk teenager one who may attempt suicide? Or one who may become a drug addict? Or one who will drop out of school? One who will steal and lie and become a criminal? What would I have done if I had consciously realised what the words 'high risk' meant? Put him on twenty-four-hour watch? Sent him to therapy? Put him into rehab? She concurs that therapy is effective for teenagers only if they want it. I have Googled 'depressed teenagers', 'signs of suicidal tendencies in teenagers' and so on and so on – and the list of bullet points seems to describe most teenagers at some time or another so is not helpful:

- Bored
- Altered sleeping patterns
- Lack of attention to personal hygiene
- Aggression
- Decline in school results, etc.

What didn't I ask his therapist? I didn't ask her if there is something I could have done differently that would have meant a different outcome. I didn't ask her if the dagga smoking helped or contributed to his suicide. I didn't ask her if he said anything about me. I didn't ask her if we'd kept him going till the age of sixteen would he then have been safe.

When I picture him in those last few months, I have to face the painful realisation that he was already dead inside – he was just going through the motions. He had given up before he'd had a chance to get going: his eyes had no expression; he didn't care; he was just pretending. He did what he had to do to get through his days, aware that when it got too much or when the opportunity presented itself he knew what he was going to do. I read that suicide is misdirected anger. Who or what was Boy so angry with that instead of killing him/her/them he killed himself? But then I'm beginning to suspect that there are as many theories on suicide as there are suicides.

35

I dreamt last night about Boy. The dream is vague – just a feeling of drowning in pain. In my dream I thought I was going mad and I would never get to recover.

I was going through my old journals – my morning pages – which I'd kept for many years on and off. I was purging, throwing out, clearing out, making way for new energy, a new me. I had taken years' worth of my paintings and chosen a handful and put them aside. The rest I burnt outside in the braai one by one. I haven't painted since Boy died – except for one portrait I tried to make of him, but I didn't finish it. I don't want to do anything I did before, and if I do, I want to do it differently, because I am not the same as I was before. I started paging through the journals wondering if I'd find something enlightening I'd written about my son. Instead I found a description of a dream I had many years ago, when Ruby-Rose was still a baby:

> I am sitting with friends and Laine socialising, and I keep asking Laine to go and check on Ruby but she ignores me. Eventually I realise I have to get up and go check on her myself. I need to find her and see that she's okay. As I walk towards where she is, I think, 'If something's happened to Ruby, it will be Laine's fault'. And I get to the bathroom and see that Ruby has drowned in the bath. I

> lift her up in my arms and carry out her limp wet body and there is a deep scream in my heart and I think, 'When I fully comprehend the enormity of this tragedy I will never be the same again', and at the same time I also think with relief, 'I am no longer responsible for parenting her'.

That was the dream. And reading about it grips my heart and chokes me because it's like it foreshadowed Boy's death. There I was at work sending SMSs to the girls saying, 'Watch your brother like a hawk', issuing instructions from my desk, telling David to take him for a drug test, but I didn't move. I was communicating with my mother, sending her messages that something's not right. I knew something wasn't right. I phoned David to get the drug test result and he said to me it's only positive for dagga, all other drugs negative, and I can't really absorb what he is saying because I have already convinced myself that Boy is using harder drugs because of his odd behaviour.

It's like I had temporary amnesia: when it finally clicks that JP is 'only' smoking dagga, I immediately forget his other behaviour. I am relieved, so relieved – I don't have to rush away from work to deal with a crisis. I can finish my day, do my interview, go home and take him out for supper and talk to him. But it won't go away – it's there at the back of my mind, that tiny voice constantly whispering, 'Why didn't you go home?' And when I repeat this story in therapy, in support groups, to friends, and so on, I am told yes, you didn't move – because you have had many crises with your children, you responded the way you always do, you didn't know he was going to kill himself. If you'd known that, you would have gone home…

And then he kills himself and I get home and I think almost the same thing: when I wake up from this nightmare I will never be the same again. And at the same time I have moments of relief or release or surrender – I never have to worry about him again, I never have to try to solve the conundrum of my son, who was elusive and distant and different – an unknown. Just when I think I get it, I get him, then he slips through my fingers and I realise I don't know him at all.

And that's what happened that fateful Thursday. It's as though I allowed him to slip through my fingers. He was a living, breathing boy – my son – and I wasn't paying attention. I wasn't paying enough attention, or the right attention – right action, the Buddhists call it – and he just slipped away. Yet, I haven't been doing all the work I've done over the past months to be so arrogant as to think I could have prevented the outcome...

If it hadn't been that day, would it have been another?

36

What is so difficult to live with is the carrying on. It's almost incomprehensible that I can carry on without a form of denial of what has happened. That's what it feels like: as though by carrying on I am denying what has happened – the enormity of it, the importance of it. As though the carrying on is saying, 'His life did not have value. See, I can carry on.' I want to scream: 'I am not carrying on because I want to – I am carrying on because I don't have a choice!' If I had a choice, I would become the mad woman in the attic. I would lose myself in the loss of him. I would move into his bedroom and get into his bed and never change the bedding so I could be close to him, his smell. I would sleep with his clothes. I would stare at his graffiti. I would scratch at his fourteen-year-old-boy detritus. I would cover his walls with images of him, his drawings and paintings. I would put his school books and his nature books neatly on the shelf, and every day I would page through them – looking, hoping, searching for a sign of something hidden that I missed the previous time for how and why this happened.

I can understand so completely why some parents leave their dead children's bedroom just as it was when the child died. Is that the real denial, I wonder? Staying put in the house with the bedroom, with everything, as it was: does that mean not facing what is? And

I am brought back to the notion of my nature – what I did give my children. There may have been plenty I didn't give, but I did give them life, and I gave them my irrepressible love of it, and my enthusiasm and energy and determination and sense of adventure.

We had fun. In between the pain and the loss, we certainly had fun. And we did stuff. John Peter saw more theatre, dance and art than any other fourteen-year-old on the planet. Did he get anything out of it – or did he just think, 'Where is she taking us now?' The last show Boy saw was just weeks before he died: Fugard's *Sizwe Banzi is Dead*. David took the kids. 'Did you enjoy it, Boy?' I asked. 'Yes,' he said. Earlier in the year, John Peter went with his sisters to *The Crucible*, which he loved, and I took him them to Lemn Sissay's one-person show *Something Dark* at the Market. Sissay tells his astonishing life story of brutality, racism, abandonment and other personal struggles and transforms them into a powerful inspirational story using poetry and humour. I took Boy because I wanted him to see this show about a man's difficult life and how Sissay used his poetry to process, express and ultimately overcome.

But of course JP didn't have a difficult life – not if looked at externally. It was all on the inside and none of us knew. Maybe it was hinted at, but we didn't really know how difficult it was to be Boy. How vulnerable, how hopeless, how pointless, how ashamed, how useless, how stupid, how ugly he must have felt. It didn't matter that we told him we loved him, that he was handsome, that I loved his drawings and any art he produced for that matter, that I admired his handiwork and appreciated him helping me – cleaning the kitchen, digging holes for plants in the garden, feeding the dogs, walking the dogs with me…

John Peter never cried – or if he did, he didn't allow me to see it. He didn't even cry when badly hurt, which was quite often. 'I think I've hurt myself,' he would say quietly, with no fuss, no drama – followed by a rush to the hospital for eight stitches to a gash in his leg or a plaster cast for a torn ligament…

He must have hidden so much, so well. He put on a face that seemed not to care but how deeply he must have felt and experienced his world. How vulnerable and desperate he must have felt. His anxiety, depression, sense of hopelessness and pain. Did he fear the future in a world where he couldn't find meaning, that he couldn't make sense of or understand? He felt like an alien – as if he didn't belong – even to us, his family who loved him so and accepted him completely. Vanessa reminded me of something I said soon after Boy died: 'He was so lucky he had David and me as parents because we accepted him so completely and didn't try to make him be somebody he wasn't.' I'd forgotten I'd said that or even felt it. I'd been so busy trying to find the causal link between my parenting and JP's suicide that I'd forgotten that he didn't kill himself because of something I did or didn't do. Rather, he lived as well as he could for the short time he was with us because he had us as parents. He probably wasn't sleeping well at night and was feeling very alone and isolated, becoming more and more disconnected each day – cut off from us and yet pretending that everything was okay. A few friends have said to me something along the lines of, 'It's easy to see where your girls come from – they come from the same mould. But how does JP fit in? He's so different from his sisters and from you and David.' And he was. There was something within him that prevented him from fitting in – and although we embraced him and his difference, even among his family he felt this difference keenly. But I don't know for sure if this is what he was feeling. I can only imagine that it was – why else would a fourteen-year-old child hang himself?

But perhaps I'm completely wrong. Maybe he was just playing, experimenting, wondering, 'What would it feel like to hang myself?' Maybe he was trying to get high. Or maybe in some corner of his heart he was ill, and perhaps he was doing the right thing considering the pain he was in – a pain that, aside from slight intimations of it, the rest of us could not comprehend.

In a way it is a gift that I have to carry on. If I didn't have three living children, and if I had enough money that I didn't have to work, the gulf would overwhelm me – I would become the gulf. I know the feeling – I have glimpses on weekends when the children are away. I become the big black hole. So in a way I have to deny what has happened because it's the only way to carry on. So denial ensures that I get up in the morning, I shower, I get dressed, I brush my teeth, I make school lunch for Ruby, I help her with her spelling, I help her get dressed. We get in the car. We start our day… another day of denial.

But with time it becomes less like denial and slowly, slowly it edges me back into life. One day I may even realise that all that superhuman effort – the effort of functioning, of getting through my days – saved me. It would be so easy to give up. I have the best excuse in the world. But I won't. I go to work and I am productive. Work saves me. Work is the only place where I can still recognise elements of the previous me. I function and some days I am even productive. I don't just want to survive. I want to live. I am determined to live.

And I take action – it helps to keep busy. After JP died I kept myself very busy making appointments for interventions for all of us, for support therapy, alternative therapy, family counselling, individual counselling, suicide-support groups, suicide therapy groups. Books, massage, flower essences, tissue salts, Rescue Remedy – you name it, I'm onto it. We try everything, hoping something will resonate and we/I will stay with it.

It is ironic that parts of his lived experience have become so much a part of my own experience since he died – alienation, isolation, disconnection, pain, depression, anxiety, meaninglessness, hopelessness. And his death presents me with an opportunity to move beyond this disconnectedness, lack of rootedness, and lack of connection with the source of life. My work is not to run away from the loss, the ache, the sorrow, but to stay with the pain even when it threatens to overwhelm to remain tender and open and kind to be connected and present to reconnect with the great source of life in a way that is real and true. That is my work.

I am learning that grief has its own language and rhythm and way…

I'm starting to feel him close by – just glimpses, moments of understanding or knowing that he is close… with me… and that no one and nothing can take that away. I can sense his outline, see his features as if I could reach out and stroke his face. I bring him close, soak him in. I lie on my bed with Ruby snuggled up next to me – and suddenly I realise he's also there.

If I still my mind long enough, and long for him enough, he materialises. Not in a psychic sense, but I can will him close. When I'm not scared, scared by the loss of him, I summon him. And although my heart aches because my rational mind knows he's gone, my heart allows him in, and it brings comfort. I am assured that I am not denying him, that I can conjure him up whenever I need to – not just the loss of him in my physical world, but the presence of him. In my heart forever…

I sat in my last suicide-support group and we shared. We reflected on the group and our expectations when we started and how it has been for us. We gave each other metaphorical gifts and we talked about how the journey has been. And then I asked the facilitators, 'How has it been for you? What did you get out of it? Are you going to facilitate more groups?' The support facilitator said, 'My daughter committed suicide', and it was as though my heart had been gripped and squeezed. I have spent hours with her and wondered who she is and why she is there and noticed how she comes in at such a different angle with her observations – like she's holding the space of the unspoken and bringing it to the surface. I can't believe she sat through eight sessions and was present for us, for me, and did not share her story. And the tears just started falling as the sadness struck me like a blow.

As I looked into her eyes, I recognised and understood the full weight and gravity of who I have become. And I felt the sorrow and anguish of all mothers who have buried a child, knowing that forever I am now one of those women. I am that sad woman who has lost a child. And I sat there helpless as the tears fell, not even making an attempt to contain them or stop them or wipe them away. I felt my pain, her pain, and in this space I didn't have to deny or pretend or put on my dark glasses. I just sat there and cried and cried and cried. I had no words. I could not explain that I was crying for my loss, and not just my loss but all loss, as the realisation of who I have become seeped into my being and my loss and I became truly acquainted. As I looked into that other mother's eyes and saw my reflection, I somehow inexplicably understood what this new relationship means. *I am you*. I am now that woman, that mother whose son killed himself. And for the first time since Boy died, I had a moment of self-pity. I have resisted this self-pity with all my being. This time I couldn't help myself.

It took some effort, but eventually I managed to pull myself back from the abyss. I directed my attention to the facilitator and asked her about her daughter.

37

At the end of 2011, about nine months after Boy died, we are in McGregor for the holidays. We get a phone call from Mike Kamstra, a gifted craftsman whom we had entrusted to make John Peter's gravestone. He tells us that the stone is ready to install. We had decided on solid concrete, and Mike added a touch of white marble to the outer layer of cement to make it smooth and to lighten, brighten and whiten it. It is a big heavy piece of concrete and we need to get quite a few men to move it. We get the stone to the grave and into its hole and pour in the stones and sand and cement and earth and concrete, under Hamish's direction. And finally it's standing there unadorned, humble and solid forever, with the words carefully carved into the concrete:

John Peter Shand Butler
19.6.1996 – 31.3.2011

The graveyard is beautiful. It is situated on the edge of the village, in a flat plain just below a krans. When I stand before Boy's grave and look up, I see the familiar purple mountains before me, and if I turn around, the Langeberg Mountains are behind me. It is still and quiet there and when the wind isn't blowing there is birdsong, big sky, veld and wild flowers. It is the perfect resting place for my son.

I need this grave, this gravestone, this place, his place, his resting place, and it gives us all somewhere to go and something to do. Whenever I am on the beach, I pick up a stone and put it in my pocket so that the next time I am in McGregor I can go and put it on Boy's grave. When we are in McGregor I can ask Ruby, 'Should we go and put a flower on your brother's grave?' and off she will run and pick a flower and down to his place we go.

As with so much after the death of my son, I want to contain it, I want to make it real, I need to place it outside of myself so that I don't explode with all the interior tumult. I want to touch and visit and see and smell. I don't just want to hold onto memories; I also want to make new ones around the loss.

When a child dies so young, it is not so much the past that is buried but the future.

John Peter wasn't on this earth long enough for us to get a sense of what his future may have been. I suspect it would have been solitary and melancholic. Slow and considered. He would have been an artist, a painter perhaps, a craftsman, potter or carpenter – or maybe a game ranger or farmer. He would have kept to himself and minded his own business, held his own counsel...

We didn't put an epitaph on his gravestone, but if we had decided to, surely it would have read, 'He was the most undemanding child'.

Afterword

Laine and Annie both read this book. Laine tells me she doesn't like how I am so hard on myself. She doesn't like that I take so much responsibility, that I blame myself. She says my self-blame feels relentless. She says to me, 'You are a great mother, the best mom. Why don't you write about that?' I tell her that I wrote the book to explore and try to understand what went wrong, not to celebrate what was right.

It's all different now. The house is sold. David and I are divorced. Ruby lives with me in a rented cottage. David lives in a rented cottage close by. Laine is at university in Grahamstown. Annie is taking a gap year in the Cape. I have found homes for the dogs. I need as little to look after as possible. My life can never be what it was. I don't want to even pretend otherwise. The chasm that Boy's death ripped through my family cannot be mended with a plaster. Instead I have to forge a new way for myself. Nothing is the same. I don't want it to be the same. A bomb went off and annihilated the landscape. It left ruin and devastation in its wake. I have a sense, though, that we, my family, are all starting to emerge from under the heavy grey, blanket of our shock and loss and grief. We are no longer the same but we are still standing. I am helpless in the enormity of it all. I am humbled. I am vulnerable. I no longer feel I can fix it. Instead, I break it down further, as if by destroying completely what was, I will somehow emerge transformed. The beautiful family I once had now seems a distant dream, a faded sepia photograph, sometimes an illusion, as if JP's death and the manner of his dying leaves me no option but to break what we were completely. I can't fix it so I tear away at it, I take great big bites out of it, I scratch at it, I throw rocks at it, I take a dagger and stab at it. I know what I am doing is destructive, but I can't help myself. I am swept up by it. I am the lava pouring out of the volcano destroying everything in its path. I want to expose my wounds. I want to nail myself to the cross. My unstable foundations are gone and there is nothing to hang on to… except my grief.

And at the same time I work so hard at my grief, I try so hard with my grief, I do everything right with my grief, I know my grief, I feel safe with my grief. I am scared that if I don't try hard enough, I will be consumed by my grief. I am afraid that if I sit still with my grief for a moment, I will never get up again. And so my grief and I keep very busy. I try and weave JP into every facet of my life, as if by hanging onto him tightly he won't disappear. I won't disappear. I went to LifeLine last week to register for their counselling course. The wise counsellor who interviewed me looked at me for a long time and then said, 'Why don't you go home and be kind to yourself?' I burst into tears and she held me. All at once I understood how hard I'd been trying instead of just being. I also knew I don't know how to be kind and gentle to myself, I don't know how to nourish myself. I said to her, 'But I don't know how.' And she answered, 'Take it easy, you don't have to do anything, stop trying so hard, just allow what has happened to sink in, take time to allow your skin to thicken.' I hear her and I know I have to spend some time now taking it easy. I need to stop pushing and achieving and acting and just breathe and be. And I can't take it on as a project, as my next task or hurdle to overcome, just gently, every day, practise mindfulness, awareness, presence. This may be the hardest part. By doing this, perhaps I will give my dear daughters licence to do the same. All that we have known is gone and now who we truly are can become – butterflies breaking out of our cocoons. Fragile, delicate, soft, beautiful and brave…

flying and landing lightly... I want for us all to find our wings and fly... like JP did.

Some days it feels as if I've come a long way. Other days not at all. Although two years have passed, this feels like the beginning. I am still reeling. Sometimes it's free fall. Occasionally I touch solid ground. I start to catch glimpses of the future. My life force is re-emerging. When I'm still enough, I can hear it calling. My heart is opening. I will find my way. I want to do lots of stuff that makes me feel alive. I want to dip into my creative well and make beautiful things. I want to see the pyramids, climb Kilimanjaro, kayak down the Orange River, swim in the sea with dolphins, skydive off Lion's Head, sleep under the stars in the Karoo, dive naked into a mountain pool, lie on the wet ground after a thunderstorm and smell the Joburg earth and drink from the puddles, I want to paint murals of colourful parrots on any old wall, I want to make more rag dolls, and I want to listen closely when my children speak. I want to do all of this because my son is dead, but I am alive. I want to reach out to others, be present to their pain. I want to show up and say yes. I want to care less what people think. I know that if I keep doing the things I love, I will eventually believe that it's okay to be me, Kate Shand.

Laine took over JP's cellphone and didn't change the voice message. So I still hear his voice when I phone and she doesn't answer. He says, 'Ah, hello, it's JP here... I'm not here... call again... later...'

David gave me a poem he wrote for John Peter in December 2012 while on a trip to Namibia – the trip he was going to take with his son:

You arrived quietly and slipped into this world
As if you had always been here,
With the eyes of a day-old sage,
You looked and didn't speak.
Eyes always darting but mouth shut,
This world you felt, with your thick hair
and thin skin.

And then one day you slipped quietly away
So as not to disturb.
Do not disturb. Do not disturb.
You took all you had been given
away with you.
You shared all you had of the small space you occupied,
and then you had no more to share.
And so you went.
We all go, when we have no more to give.
So we don't feel the pain,
of chunks of us being bitten out of us.
You could no more.

And now in this vast landscape,
of this massive continent,
you take up an even smaller space,
that is forever yours.
– David Butler, the Kalahari, December 2012

Glossary

bloukappie	an indigenous shrub
bossie	a small bush or shrub
Builders Warehouse	a building and homeware store
Checkers	a local supermarket chain
dagga	marijuana
doring tree	thorn tree
Game	a South African household and appliance store
garage	South African term for petrol station
Grade R/Grade O	preschool, before first grade
Joburg Gen	State hospital also known as Charlotte Maxeke
jol	a party or to party
krans	a sheer rock face
laatlammetjie	youngest child of a family, born to older parents
legavaan	rock monitor, a large southern African monitor lizard
leiwatersloot	irrigation water channels
Mail & Guardian	a weekly newspaper
Market	The Market Theatre in Newtown, Johannesburg

Mxit	a South African social network chat line
onderdorp	literally, the 'undertown'
Pirates	a Johannesburg sports club
potjie	stew, traditionally cooked in a round, three-legged, cast iron pot on a fire
RAPS	Repertory Amateur Players Society, a society that promotes the amateur movement in South Africa
SACS	South African College Schools, an established junior school for boys
SANCA	South African National Council on Alcoholism and Drug Dependence
SMS	short message service, text messaging
stoep	veranda
Stopayne	an over-the-counter painkiller
tik	Crystal Methamphetamine
toktokkie	a dark, round beetle
UCT	University of Cape Town
veld	wild fields

Respects

When we are in matric, Kate phones me and says, 'You'll never guess who I met last night... David Butler.' David, a well-known actor in Cape Town, looks like a young Robert Redford. Kate is beautiful, clever, talented, and together they are perfect. Growing up, I had spent many weekends in Kate's home. Her mother always had time to help us make a matric dance dress or curl our hair. Later I also get to know David's wonderful family.

We spend our twenties visiting the Old Mill Lodge in McGregor, swimming in the dam, eating bread baked by Kate's father, dancing in the *onderdorp*. Kate has a red hibiscus in her long black hair. David has on his panama hat and they are dancing together. A photo is taken; they look so happy.

Kate is so grown-up with her babies, her husband and her house with wooden floors. Everything she does, she does well. She cooks delicious meals, together with David reupholsters a chair, sews, paints and works. Like a graceful dancer, Kate has the knack of making it all look effortless. With his rich voice and mesmerising presence, David is a celebrated actor, yet modest and unaffected. There is a kindness, hospitality and incredible warmth in the Butler-Shand home. David's delightful sister Rosalind and I play with the babies and we all hang out in Rockey Street in Yeoville.

As you walk into the Berea house, there is an exquisite mosaic floor that leads into a long dark passage. Kate and David have bashed open a door and put in a window to let the light stream through. There is a lot of laughter. It's a space where people are accepted for who they are. Both David and Kate are romantics, poets at heart, free spirits, good, intelligent and thoughtful people. They are givers, in every sense of the word. Their home is filled with books, photographs, paintings, food, jars of olives, home-made jams, coffee, their Staffie Tucker, family and friends – lots of friends. David has an awesome record collection. When the needle touches the vinyl, the dancing begins.

Kate phones me twice a week to say, 'We're having roasted chicken [or some other tempting dish] tonight, you must come for supper.' A poet friend comments on the way David braais a fish with such tenderness and care. Under their bed are posters of David's shows and the matric paintings he did. Every year Kate frames another one of the paintings or posters for his birthday.

A magazine publishes a series of photographs called 'What I'm doing before 10:00 a.m.' The series includes a black and white picture of David. He is sitting on the stoep steps, feeding his beloved baby boy a bottle. Their Berea home has a huge lemon tree in the front garden. Whenever I visit, I pick a lemon. There is enough fruit for everyone. It's a place where people want to be. And what came after doesn't change what was. A beautiful family, who adored their beautiful boy. A boy who came into the world at home and left the world at home, surrounded by people who loved him.

Vanessa Levenstein
Cape Town
November 2012

Letter to Boy

Dear John Peter

Moving into your home and connecting with your family after your departure put me in an environment where I experienced nothing but an outpouring of love. Total honesty presented herself; there was only the aching rawness of fully felt pain. And with that total honesty and acceptance came love. John Peter, your marked and deliberate absence caused waves to break out from our hitherto contained, hardened hearts. Whoever heard of the courage of your parting was first completely numb and then moved to the deepest sorrow and concern. With each expression of the sorrow felt and remembered, waves lifted and moved outwards, touching everyone in their wake. And in that space was the deepest, most profound love. Everyone became that. Everyone merged into their natural state. There was raw reality – with total acceptance.

The few people I have seen in McGregor since my return have spoken to me of how this event has changed their lives, how resistance to things has just melted away. So many candles were lit in the village over the week of your death and there was this absolute surge of love. Wherever one looked, everyone was in a heightened state of consciousness, aware of each potent moment.

Your blessed mother, even in the deepest sorrow, would still catch herself out. She would say something like 'I should do...' and then immediately stop herself and say, 'No, I want to do...' In the deepest grief, her mind was controlled and observant, not subject to unconscious tyranny.

No one stops when a child is born. There is, of course, a celebration, but you don't stop what you are doing when a friend gives birth. Birth does not carry the gift of the introspection that sorrow demands of one. Your departure stopped us all in our tracks, midstream. There was no way anyone could step aside from the rising wave of emotions. Your death broke my heart right open. My internal jaded cynic fled upon seeing the light. I am sad that so many will have a hard time adjusting to you appearing only in memory now. And yet I am so profoundly grateful for what IT has produced. In this world, sinking, shaking and warring, your decision led to wave upon wave of love and clarity of spirit. A bright light in the darkness.

Seeing the grace and wisdom with which this family has met your death has inspired a new way of perceiving for many. To allow that deepest sorrow and in turn meet an inner peace – this is probably the greatest challenge given to a human. Between the waves of loss and regret, to respect your decision and just continue to feel the love of this being in his eternal presence. The acceptance of those close to you and its effect that has unfolded with your unorthodox journey is my most profound blessing to date. Thank you, John Peter. Angel Boy. It became apparent by the last thing found of yours – a list – that you wanted to go into the wild and survive. You wanted to hunt and grow and live off the thriving land, leave the hallowed city – and when you saw that to get to the land would be more than you could do, you chose the next route – away from this clumsy, heavy lifestyle we are all wrapped up in.

From the beautiful falling rain and the embrace of your home, I return to the kingdom of sunlight. Sitting in the garden watching the mousebirds have what sounds like a parents-teachers meeting, the chickens clucking, the light filtering through the banana leaves, the occasional ant crawling on my arm, the wasp stinging and dragging the rain spider to her lair. And in the midst of this – you are present.

With much gratitude and respect, John Peter, respect.

Susannah Huntley
McGregor
11 April 2011